WINNING
MONOPOLY

WINNING
MONOPOLY

A Complete Guide to Property Accumulation,
Cash Flow Strategy, and Negotiating Techniques
When Playing the Best-selling Board Game

KAZ DARZINSKIS

HARPER & ROW, PUBLISHERS, NEW YORK
Cambridge, Philadelphia, San Francisco, Washington
London, Mexico City, São Paulo, Singapore, Sydney

WINNING MONOPOLY. Copyright © 1987 by Kaz Darzinskis. All rights reserved. Printed in the United States of America. No part of this book may be used or reproduced in any manner whatsoever without written permission except in the case of brief quotations embodied in critical articles and reviews. For information address Harper & Row, Publishers, Inc., 10 East 53rd Street, New York, N.Y. 10022. Published simultaneously in Canada by Fitzhenry & Whiteside Limited, Toronto.

FIRST EDITION
Designer: Helene Berinsky
Copyeditor: Bruce Emmer

Library of Congress Cataloging-in-Publication Data
Darzinskis, Kaz.
   Winning Monopoly.
   1. Monopoly (Game)   I. Title.
GV1469.M65D37   1987   794.2   86-46054
ISBN 0-06-096127-9 (pbk.)

87 88 89 90 91 MPC 10 9 8 7 6 5 4 3 2 1

To Debbie.

Mrs. Lee Dennis, Curator of the Game Preserve, Peterborough, New Hampshire, and Professor Ralph Anspach of San Francisco State University provided insights into the early history of Monopoly and Monopoly-like games. Various members of Parker Brothers headquarters staff in Beverly, Massachusetts, helped interpret certain subtleties about the rules. My wife, Deborah, provided literary feedback and, more important, great patience. A less supportive observer might have concluded my work was simply a way to play games, play more games, and play ever yet more games.

Contents

Preface

At first it seemed appropriate to persuade readers of this book that I was truly an expert at winning Monopoly. But faster than I could recall my won-lost record, I realized it would be a wasted effort. Winning Monopoly involves luck as well as skill, so who could be sure I haven't simply enjoyed more than my share of luck—especially since I've lost Monopoly to persons who would never dream of themselves as Monopoly experts.

I decided, instead, to promote myself as a long-time Monopoly *fanatic*. The main difference between a fanatic and an expert is that experts are paid, while fanatics "work" for nothing.

Only a Monopoly fanatic like myself could remember his first Monopoly game over 30 years ago. In the summer of 1955 Eisenhower was president, the radio played big band music or novelty songs, and the lady next door invited my sister and me to join her two kids in their house for a game of Monopoly.

Dave, the oldest in the group, had played before and directed the game. When he first landed on Income Tax, he declared, "We don't play that square." What a relief! Though old enough to read what the square said, I had no idea what "10 percent" meant. You had to reach fourth grade to learn percents.

I don't remember who won that first game, but I'm pretty sure I didn't.

The way youngsters look at time, it was a long time before Monopoly again became a memorable activity. When I was 10 or

11, I became caught in a wave of Monopoly enthusiasm at my uncle's house.

Uncle Nick and his wife played Monopoly often—so often that they did not have to count the squares or look at the Title Deed cards to determine the rents. Players' tokens virtually flew around the board; in fact, their Monopoly board had grooves in it where the tokens landed.

This whirlwind style of play meant that I could lose three games within the same time most people lost only once.

Learning anything comes quickly at age 10 or 11, and armed with a thorough understanding of percents and other elements of arithmetic, I quickly learned everything I thought there was to know about Monopoly rules and about what it takes to win the game.

Not satisfied with playing Monopoly only at my uncle's house, I convinced my parents to get a Monopoly set of our own. Fascinated by the game and virtually unbeatable when I played against my little sisters, I dreamed up ways to make the game even better.

I toiled many hours devising my own "improved" version of the game. Using taped-together pieces of cardboard, I invented additional properties players could land on and buy. On my "Monopoly" board there were properties so costly that Boardwalk seemed cheap by comparison.

Occasionally I was able to coerce my sisters into playing my new, improved version of Monopoly, but the rest of the world was unimpressed. I learned that Monopoly was useless unless others joined in to play. Looking back, I find some consolation in the fact that the failure of my own Monopoly game saved me from facing a trademark infringement lawsuit.

Up through high school I played Monopoly with my childhood chums, Nino and Vyt, but when we went off to different colleges, I temporarily lost the Monopoly habit.

Soon after college, however, we were all back in the same part of the country. Nino and Vyt both married, but every so often they negotiated a Friday night away from their wives, and we gathered at one of our homes to play a Monopoly game or two while chugging down huge quantities of pizza and beer.

Our Monopoly nights out were among the very best of times, but eventually my most reliable Monopoly partners became caught up in the various things married men get involved in, and our

Monopoly nights out became increasingly rare. Also, our aging bodies became less tolerant of the calories and alcohol that our style of Monopoly play involved.

Still a bachelor, I wound up spending much of my free time at a singles club. One of the events the singles club sponsored was a Friday night "games night." Games nights involved going to a hall and bringing a game that others would join in to play. Of course, I always brought my Monopoly set, and, happily, four, five, or more fellow singles always joined to play the game.

This episode of my Monopoly-playing career was unlike all the others: I always won. And I do mean always. The number of players in these games made it unlikely that I was simply enjoying a string of good luck. I wondered whether I had finally learned the game well enough to always win or whether my playing partners were simply concentrating on other things.

Getting married eventually ended my winning ways at the singles club, but not my interest in Monopoly. To my surprise, I married a woman who did not enjoy playing Monopoly (at least not when I was in the game). But she did allow me the freedom to spend countless hours in my den, facing a computer monitor and programming Monopoly subroutines.

I spent almost a year programming a computer to simulate how logical, thinking humans of absolutely equal ability play Monopoly. It was a big job because numerous factors come into play each time a Monopoly player makes a decision. Each decision factor had to be put in a detailed overall logic diagram to form a type of artificial intelligence. Finally, the artificial intelligence had to be translated into computer code.

It is amazing to me how much time and high-tech wizardry was necessary to "teach" the computer to do the same thing that I learned to do for myself so easily when I was 7 years old.

The payoff from this effort was that with the computer I could play Monopoly more often than ever before, and I could play endlessly. The computer could play Monopoly and collect data from those games even while I slept. And it could do so faster than any group of humans that ever picked up a Community Chest card.

With the computer, I've played and analyzed over 187,000 full-length Monopoly games, not including several hundred played just for fun. If Parker Brothers ever runs a contest for Monopoly-playing enthusiasm, I am going to submit my name right away.

One night after I had been running the computer for a few months, Deb, my wife, came to the den to see what I was doing. I told her that I had learned that a great deal of randomness was apparent in the relative rankings of players in four-player games. In other words, there is a lot of luck involved. She said everybody knew that and was puzzled as to why I needed to sit in front of a computer for months to learn what was obvious to everyone else in the world.

I had not given her a complete explanation, however, because what I had learned, at least from my standpoint, was very sad. The correlation coefficients the computer spat out showed that although the winner of a Monopoly game was predictable, the order of bankruptcy for the losing players was not. That meant that the final standings of the losers are due to pure blind luck.

When talking about skill in Monopoly, there are only two meaningful standings: the winner and the nonwinner. Second place is no more meritorious than fifth place.

All those times that I congratulated myself for coming in second in a five-player game, I could have been congratulating myself for nothing except being lucky. How sad!

Although I learned about the relative importance of luck and skill, my main purpose in studying Monopoly was to identify what winners do differently from losers. I was looking for winning advantages, especially advantages that few players appreciate. When I found one I wrote it down, and those notes later served as the basis for this book.

Initially, my only purpose with the computer Monopoly project was to help me win more often. Winning has been important to me, because it is more fun than losing, and since the purpose of the game is to have fun, it has always seemed sensible to try to win. Being fanatical about winning Monopoly is identical to being fanatical about having fun.

Winning is not all there is to having fun, however. The quality of play matters too, and to have a truly good game it is necessary to have knowledgeable playing partners. So even though putting this book in the hands of opponents will make it harder for me to win, routinely having good-quality games will be easier.

Perhaps the best thing about winning Monopoly games is to avoid losing to particular people. More than other games, Monopoly opponents are largely people to whom you especially do not want to lose. Examples include new players, one's spouse, younger siblings, and one's own kids. I think going through the effort to learn about winning Monopoly is worthwhile if it avoids only one such embarrassing loss.

Monopoly does not have the reputation of an intellectual game like chess, because luck is involved in Monopoly. But that is precisely why the game deserves study. To win Monopoly consistently, it is not only necessary to outmaneuver opponents but also do so thoroughly enough to outweigh shortages of luck all players occasionally encounter.

That is why this book has a seemingly endless list of winning tips, both major and minor. It may seem like overkill, but as someone who once landed on Income Tax four times in a row, I know it is impossible to be too fanatical about finding ways to defeat my playing partners. Extra, reserve firepower is necessary to overcome those occasional games in which Lady Luck sides only with opponents!

PART ONE

SET UP THE GAME TO
SET UP OPPONENTS

As for most of the world's great games, it took many years for Monopoly to evolve into the game we know today. Real estate rent games have been played in England for over 100 years. In the United States, "The Monopolist," a game involving money, debt, and bankruptcy, was introduced in 1885.

In the early part of this century producing Monopoly-like games was a minor cottage industry. In a number of U.S. cities along the Eastern Seaboard, groups of players copied gameboards by hand and published their own rules. The street names were usually taken from the players' hometowns. Today's version of Monopoly thus benefited from the collective wisdom of generations of game players, many of whom proposed and tested changes in the game. Later players were free to accept or reject the changes based on whether a change made the game better or not.

Elizabeth Magie Phillips, who lived, appropriately, in Virginia and Illinois, was the first to patent a Monopoly-like game. During the Depression in the early 1930s Monopoly began to enjoy some commercial success. A company in Indianapolis sold a game called "Finance" that today would be recognized as Monopoly. At the same time, Charles B. Darrow, the person best known in connection with Monopoly, was producing and selling the game in Philadelphia and New York.

During this period, three of that day's major game producers, Milton-Bradley, Selchow and Righter, and Parker Brothers, were all asked to publish the game but declined the offers.

Around 1935 Parker Brothers reversed itself and, in separate deals, bought the rights to Monopoly from the Indianapolis company, from Elizabeth Magie Phillips, and from Charles B. Darrow. Parker Brothers, in effect, purchased a monopoly on Monopoly.

In the 50 years since Monopoly became widely available, the game has spread to 33 countries. It is now played by over 250 million people. The more than 90 million sets sold thus far have contained more Monopoly money than all the real currency in circulation in the United States today.

Monopoly's long history and great popularity cause some problems with the rules. Although the rules have remained virtually unchanged for over 50 years, many groups of players have adopted variations of the rules and special conventions. You do not have to leave the country to find Monopoly in different style than yours—a trip across your neighborhood is probably sufficient.

Twists in the rules that Monopoly's long history have helped create do not have to be problems. Part One of this book shows how to use opponents' quirks about rules to improve your chances to win.

1

Monopoly Traditions

Whether among friends, family, or new acquaintances, it has been common for over 50 years for someone to enliven a gathering instantly by simply saying, "Hey, let's play Monopoly."

And it is unlikely anybody in the room will ask, "What's Monopoly?" Monopoly is one of those things, like riding a bicycle, that nearly everyone learns to do.

As would be expected for any activity so old and so widespread, Monopoly has formed a set of expected practices and traditions. As Monopoly is played in a group setting, it is wise to follow these traditions.

IT'S YOUR TURN—ROLL THE DICE

The first tradition is not to spend a lot of time during your turn making decisions or wondering what to do. By no means should you bring a calculator or a book of statistical formulas to the playing table—even a pad and pencil are out of line.

Monopoly play is governed more by gut feelings and intuition than by mathematical thinking or objective analysis. The intuition used by Monopoly players comes mostly from previous experiences watching or playing the game.

There is no way to avoid reliance on intuition in Monopoly, nor is it desirable to do so. Many decisions in Monopoly involve so many factors that calculating the results of alternative actions would be unbearably complicated and time-consuming. It would destroy the fun of the game.

This book does not suggest fundamentally changing the way you play Monopoly. Monopoly will always remain an instinctive game. This book contains no complicated mathematical formulas to learn, no list of numbers to memorize, no charts to refer to in the middle of a game.

Instead, this book aims to help you improve your instincts for the game. Most of the early chapters address how to pull in more cash than your opponents. Later chapters address how to recognize and acquire the most powerful monopoly in any particular game, in order to drive opponents into bankruptcy. In short, this book will develop your instincts for, first, earning cash and, second, investing your cash.

As often as not, playing Monopoly is an unplanned event, so it would often not be possible to rely on charts, formulas, or even a handy copy of this book. You are liable to play your next game of Monopoly at a friend's house, when all such aids are back at home.

PAY ATTENTION TO PEOPLE, NOT CARDBOARD

Not only are lengthy, complicated considerations not part of the Monopoly tradition, but they could be self-defeating. Monopoly has two sides, the gameboard and the human side, and neither should be neglected.

A Monopoly player whose attention is directed at making long calculations is liable to neglect the human factors. If you fail to read and understand your opponents, you could lose any advantages you originally hoped to gain by making all those calculations.

DO NOT BE TOO SERIOUS

Monopoly is not played in the no-nonsense, intense atmosphere common to chess or bridge. Monopoly is played in a light, patter-filled ambiance. The game requires continuous talking, if only to ask for rents or for change from the Banker. This leads to an informal and relaxing atmosphere, making possible and even encouraging playing the game while nibbling on pretzels or sipping a beverage. At times Monopoly can be so casual that a player might leave to change records on the stereo while opponents move his token and manage his money.

It is a good idea to adopt Monopoly's light mood, because such an atmosphere, according to psychologists, is the best one for stimulating creativity. Creativity is important to winning, because it helps Monopoly players routinely fashion some of the most unusual deals ever seen on earth.

Keeping the atmosphere light and creative is most important during those critical portions of the game when deals are struck to form monopolies. Professional negotiators say you are more likely to succeed in negotiations when the other side is relaxed and comfortable. When bargaining, it pays to be mentally tough and emotionally cheerful and relaxed.

At the critical stages of the game, it may be necessary to become quite ruthless in negotiating a trade or deal. Your chances of winning as well as Monopoly tradition demand that in such situations you combine ruthlessness with a happy smile. In this sense, Monopoly trades can be a bit dirty—if they are done right.

COOPERATE!

Go to any major library and you can find a number of books about noncompetitive sports and games. These books are for people who believe that children should not be exposed to any activities involving competition. Noncompetitive game advocates have promoted a version of Monopoly aimed at promoting cooperation among players.

Anyone who believes that Monopoly needs an added dose of cooperation does not appreciate how to win the game. Almost every game of Monopoly involves trades and deals, and every trade or deal involves an element of cooperation. Only each player's self-interest prevents cooperation from growing into an alliance.

Without cooperation, Monopoly tends to fall into an endless stalemate. Only occasionally do players prefer to play for hour after hour like robots, counting up the hours and the thousands of dollars accumulated. New world records for continuous play are usually of little interest. What most players truly want to do is gain control of the board while forcing every opponent into irreversible bankruptcy, thus becoming the lone survivor and uncontested victor. To win Monopoly, be ready to cooperate!

INVITE EVERYONE

It is Monopoly tradition that everyone can join in to play. Kids can play in the same game with the older folks, because Monopoly tolerates wide-ranging skill levels. For example, without alternative monopoly prospects, both beginner and expert will do the same thing when landing on an unowned Boardwalk square: buy it. On most moves of a player's token, there is actually no decision at all to make. You simply do what the rules require.

Among bona fide games of skill, Monopoly is rather unique in this regard. You do not, for example, expect to find a 7-year-old playing a serious game of poker with adults, nor do you expect to find someone new to chess defeating an experienced player. In Monopoly, by contrast, you can have a good game with nearly anybody.

If you want to maximize the number of opponents you force into bankruptcy, conform to the tradition and pull everyone into the game. It is easier to defeat six opponents in a seven-player game than it is to defeat them separately in two four-player games.

Once your playing skills have developed to the extent that you win the majority of games you play, you may gain satisfaction from inviting into Monopoly even people you do not particularly like!

THE FIRST FIVE WINNING ADVANTAGES

In this book the major points to help win Monopoly are presented as "strategic advantages" or "tactical advantages."

The winning tips from this chapter are all simple: follow the five monopoly traditions.

* **STRATEGIC ADVANTAGE 1:** Make decisions quickly. Long bouts of indecision can antagonize fellow players.

∗ STRATEGIC ADVANTAGE 2: Pay attention to your opponents; concentrating solely on the gameboard can result in unrecognized opportunities and unpleasant surprises.

∗ STRATEGIC ADVANTAGE 3: Contribute toward maintaining a light, chatty, and relaxed atmosphere.

∗ STRATEGIC ADVANTAGE 4: Adopt a cooperative attitude toward your opponents.

∗ STRATEGIC ADVANTAGE 5: Invite all to play.

2 🚂

The Right Game

To win Monopoly you must first figure out which game you are playing and then insist on playing one game at a time. This probably sounds silly, but these are real problems.

One difficulty you are liable to face is that your opponents will want to switch from one game to another in midstream. Just as it is difficult to shoot a bull's-eye when you cannot see the target, winning Monopoly is hard to do if the rules change in the middle of the game.

There are four distinct sets of Monopoly rules. In addition to regular Monopoly played according to the basic, long set of rules, there are rules for three types of short Monopoly games (see Figure 2.1).

The four sets of rules are of themselves not a problem, because all the games are similar, and if you know how to win the basic, long game, you know how to win any of them.

The danger is that some of your opponents may try to mix up or combine the four separate sets of Monopoly rules into one hybrid game, which you may not be able to win.

HOW TO RECOGNIZE THE HYBRID GAME

A hybrid game combines the rules from the basic, long rules (Game 1) with the rules for Game 2, 3, or 4. One particular hybrid game stands out as having gained wide acceptance. It would be descriptive to call it the long, short game.

To play the long, short game you play at first under basic, long rules. If eventually it becomes clear that no one will go bankrupt and the game will continue indefinitely, the players agree to an arranged cutoff time when they tabulate everyone's assets and declare the richest player the winner.

Many Monopoly players find it hard to accept that this is a hybrid. Nevertheless, there is absolutely no provision in the basic, long rules for determining a winner when there is more than one player left in a game. The basic, long rules read: "A bankrupt player

---

┌──────────────┤ FIGURE 2.1 ├──────────────┐

RULES FOR BASIC, LONG MONOPOLY AND THREE SHORT GAMES

Game 1: Basic Long Rules

These are the original, four-page rules provided with every Monopoly set. Most players assume that this is the set of rules that applies unless agreed otherwise before the game.

Game 2: Short Game A

Printed on a leaflet inside all sets, this game's rules are based on Game 1 but feature four major changes: Some Title Deed cards are dealt out as in a card game, there are three houses per lot instead of four, the game ends when the second player goes bankrupt, and the richest player wins.

Game 3: Short Game B

Found on the reverse side of the leaflet with rules for Short Game A, this game also deals out some of the Title Deed cards and provides for a preagreed time limit when assets are totaled and the richest player wins.

Game 4: Tournament Monopoly

This game has a 90-minute time limit. Properties are bought normally; the richest player after 90 minutes wins. The rules for this game are not supplied with Monopoly sets but are distributed at sanctioned Monopoly tournaments.

└──┘

must immediately retire from the game. The last player left in the game wins." That is all it says about winning and losing—no buts, ifs, or ands. First place belongs to the surviving player; second place belongs, presumably, to the last to go bankrupt; third place to the next to last to go bankrupt; and so on.

Basic, long Monopoly provides only two alternatives: force all but the last player into bankruptcy, or play on forever. To finish a Monopoly game and to crown a winner, the players must assemble at least one killer monopoly, a monopoly with rents high enough to cause bankruptcies.

TRADING IS A BUILT-IN FEATURE

This situation was certainly not an oversight. The possibility of a stalemate was included purposely.

The purpose was to force players to trade with each other. In other words, the purpose was to force players to "manufacture" monopolies. Forced trading is how Monopoly induces players to

FIGURE 2.2

FREQUENCY OF KILLER* MONOPOLIES FOR ALL MONOPOLY GAMES

	8	7	6	5	4	3	2
Number of players	8	7	6	5	4	3	2
Number of killer monopolies	3938	486	312	882	1572	1193	4314
Games	37847	3581	1727	3654	4293	1597	3317
Players gaining natural killer monopoly as a percent of all players	1.0	1.9	3.0	4.8	9.1	24.9	65.0

Data based on results of 55,963 games.

* Killer monopolies include all but the Baltic, Utility, and Railroad monopolies.

deal with each other rather than simply to manipulate inanimate objects.

Everyone prefers a game that has a conclusion and a chance to win. Figure 2.2 shows that when more than two people play Monopoly, it is unlikely that any player will get a monopoly naturally, that is, simply by rolling the dice. In the vast majority of Monopoly games there are no monopolies unless players manufacture them by trading. For example, in five-player games, your chance of a natural killer monopoly is only about 1 in 20.

During Monopoly's early years, the rules did not allow for two-player games, the only type of Monopoly that usually yields killer monopolies naturally. Provision for a two-player game was added later.

HOW TO AVOID STALEMATES

Despite the strong incentive to start negotiating and get the game moving, groups of players will occasionally find themselves unable to agree on any trades leading to monopolies. When this happens, it usually means that one or more of the players have in the back of their minds the possibility of winning the game by becoming the richest player.

> ∗ **STRATEGIC ADVANTAGE 6:** If no one but you seems willing to trade, check your partners' understanding of the rules to make certain they understand that there is no winner in a stalemated game. Imparting the correct understanding will often cause players to deal or trade to avoid a stalemated, no-win game.

WHY HYBRID MONOPOLY IS NOT "REAL MONOPOLY"

Switching from the basic, long rules to the rules for one of the short games truly is like switching to an entirely different game.

The idea behind the basic, long Monopoly rules is to assemble and develop powerful monopolies to push opposing players into bankruptcy, whereas the idea behind the short games is to maximize cash on hand. These games require very different tactics to win.

THE BIRTH OF MONOPOLY CONFUSION

Why is it possible for some players to succeed when they demand changing the rules by which the winner is determined? The answer is that there is genuine confusion about how to play Monopoly.

Monopoly players usually learn to play not by reading the rules but by playing or watching others play the game. Feeling that they already know the game, many Monopoly players never bother to read the official rules. Thus deviations from the written rules, whether intentional or not, can end up being accepted as gospel.

TACTICS AND STRATEGY

In this book the various smarter playing decisions you make to become wealthier (jail-stay duration, income tax, trading individual properties) are called tactics. The ideas you use to assemble and build more powerful monopolies than your opponents are called strategies.

A richest-player-wins game of Monopoly is predominantly a tactical game; basic, long Monopoly contains both tactical and strategic elements, so skilled players can exercise their strategic skills better in basic, long Monopoly. Tactical, short games involve a greater element of luck in determining the winner.

It is in the winning interest of skilled players to insist on playing by the basic, long rules from the beginning of the game to the end. Rather than switch rules to end a knotted game, declare a stalemate.

> **✳ STRATEGIC ADVANTAGE 7:** Insist on playing by the basic, long rules throughout the game, if those are the rules under which you began the game.

If someone insists on counting his or her assets at the end of a stalemated game, it is not necessary to try to prevent it. Simply return your own money and Title Deed cards to the bank uncounted. The winner thus remains undetermined as the rules specify.

WHEN TO ACCEPT A SWITCH TO SHORT-GAME RULES

Suppose there were a way to know with confidence who would be the richest player in a long, stalemated game. If you could be sure that you would be the richest, you could happily accept a switch to a richest-player-wins game. If you knew the opposite to be true, you could continue to resist the switch in rules. Fortunately, it is possible to predict the future of many Monopoly games.

Chapter 18 shows how to predict quickly and accurately the relative wealth of every player in any game without killer monopolies, that is, without monopolies that can cause opponents to go bankrupt.

   * STRATEGIC ADVANTAGE 8: Before agreeing to switch rules to any game other than basic, long Monopoly, predict your final standing using the I2 wealth predictor described in Chapter 18.

   * STRATEGIC ADVANTAGE 9: Agree to switch to the richest-player-wins short game only if the final standings predictor indicates that you will finish as the wealthiest player.

A richest-player-wins rule does not result in the most exciting game, but a win is a win. There can be some satisfaction for you in watching everyone grind through an "actionless" game while you alone know that everyone's efforts will culminate in a win for you.

3 ⚒

Monopoly Myths

Monopoly myths are mythical rules by which to play Monopoly—rules that are unwritten, unofficial, and at odds with the published rules. Monopoly myths are basically homemade rules, though they are accepted by millions of players, many of whom will swear that they first learned them by reading the rules from their Monopoly set.

Consider yourself a very unusual Monopoly player if you have never subscribed to one or more of the myths described here.

It is useful to know about Monopoly myths because some of them weaken your chances of winning.

MONOPOLY REFERENCES

Reading the following list, you may have difficulty accepting that all are myths. Therefore, I have provided references: paragraph letters and line numbers corresponding to sequential paragraphs and lines in the official rules that came with your Monopoly set. You can use these references to assure yourself that the myths are indeed myths.

MYTHICAL RULES THAT REWARD LUCK

If you are an above-average player or plan to be one, it is to your advantage to play by the rules that play on skill and to avoid those that reward blind luck. Following is a list of such mythical rules.

MONOPOLY MYTH 1: *If no one goes bankrupt after a long period of play, the richest player wins.*

This myth was fully explained in Chapter 2. The richest player does not win except when playing by one of the short-game rules. Standings of players are determined by the order in which they go bankrupt. Without bankruptcies there are no winners.

MONOPOLY MYTH 2: *Trading properties is not allowed by the rules.*

Actually, the rules encourage trading (A11, S14). Convincing evidence that trading is allowed comes from the box in which Monopoly sets are packaged. The box says it contains "real estate trading game equipment." The introduction to the rules states: "The game is one of shrewd and amusing trading and excitement."

MONOPOLY MYTH 3: *It is illegal to trade properties if new monopolies will be formed.*

This is a corollary of Myth 2, and it is a myth for the same reasons.

MONOPOLY MYTH 4: *You may give the bank mortgaged property instead of cash if you owe money to the bank and do not have enough cash to pay.*

Not a widely followed myth, this one began, of all places, in a 1974 book about Monopoly. This mythical rule would definitely violate some of the sections of the bankruptcy rules (T15) and would make it virtually impossible ever to go bankrupt to the bank. Furthermore, this myth would actually reward players who have the "luck" to go bankrupt to the bank rather than to fellow players.

According to rule T18, "If a player owes the bank more than he can pay, he must turn over all his assets to the bank."

To stay in the game, you must get enough cash to pay your debt to the bank by dealing with another player.

MONOPOLY MYTH 5: *If a player goes bankrupt to the bank (as opposed to going bankrupt to a fellow player), the bank holds the properties of the bankrupt player until a surviving player lands on the property and elects to buy it.*

The rules on this point (T15) are clear. The bank takes possession of a bankrupt player's properties but immediately puts them up for auction.

MONOPOLY MYTH 6: *Double the rent if you land on someone's back, that is, if you land on a lot on which an opponent's token already rests.*

Some players play a variation of this variation: pay no rent if you land on someone's back. The rules clearly state that more than one player's token may occupy a single property square. What a player does when landing on a property is unaffected by whether another player's token is already on the square (E7).

MYTHICAL RULES THAT KILL DECISION MAKING

The following mythical rules are disadvantageous to skilled players because they kill opportunities to make decisions or judgments, thus aiding the unskilled player.

MONOPOLY MYTH 7: *Players may substitute beans, buttons, checkers, or other objects for houses or hotels if the latter are in short supply.*

This may or may not be legal. The rules specify that there are supposed to be 12 hotels and 32 houses (B4). Substitutes for Monopoly houses can be used as long as the substitute houses and the original houses do not add up to more than 32.

MONOPOLY MYTH 8: *You can negotiate about trades and deals only during particular times.*

The Monopoly rules contain no "gag orders." It is permissible to negotiate at any time. This is consistent with the main intent of the rules, which are structured to promote trading between players without actually commanding them to do so.

MONOPOLY MYTH 9: *To determine your income tax, count up all cash on hand and multiply that by 10 percent.*

The rules are very specific about what to do to calculate income tax liability. You have to pay income tax on your total assets—not just cash. You must pay income tax on the value of all property owned, including houses and the full face value of mortgaged lots.

INCOME
TAX
•
PAY 10%
OR
$200

MONOPOLY MYTH 10: *Upon landing on Income Tax, the player should add up the dollar value of all assets and pay either 10 percent of total assets or $200, whichever turns out to be less.*

Actually, the Monopoly rules intend the player to decide whether to pay $200 or 10 percent of all assets *before* he adds up the dollar value of his assets. Therefore, it is possible for a player to decide to pay 10 percent of assets, find he has assets over $2000, and wind up owing the bank more than $200 in income tax (T12, T13, T14).

MONOPOLY MYTH 11: *You cannot collect rent while you are in jail.*

One sentence in the rules reads: "A player may buy and erect a house, sell or buy property, and collect rentals even though he is in jail." Not allowing a player to collect rents while in jail would virtually force all players to pay $50 immediately to get out of jail early. Following the rule as written gives a player a serious decision to make after landing in jail (H1, M25).

LUXURY
TAX

PAY $75.00

MONOPOLY MYTH 12: *It is illegal to negotiate deals involving the rights or obligations of Chance or Community Chest cards, immunities for owned properties, options, rights, and so on.*

Actually any kind of deal is legal as long as every player involved meets his or her obligation to the bank and as long as the deal does not involve a loan of money or the sale of houses or hotels from one player to another (U1, R1). Deals to pay another player's Chance card liabilities or Luxury Tax obligations are examples of strange but legal deals.

MONOPOLY MYTH 13: *You can sell a "get out of jail free" card to the bank for $50.*

This so-called rule probably came about because the "get out of jail" card is worth $50 at some point in time. However, the present value of money spent in the future is always less than the face amount, so a "get out of jail" card is worth something less than $50.

It is always possible for a player to go bankrupt or for the game to end before the holder of the card lands in jail again, in which case the card was worth nothing. The rules (J5) state that the card may be sold by one player to another player at a price agreeable to both, but it does not give a player permission to sell it to the bank.

✳ **TACTICAL ADVANTAGE 1:** Use any "get out of jail free" card that you obtain at first opportunity. If the card goes unused, it represents a waste of $50.

✳ **TACTICAL ADVANTAGE 2:** Never pay more than $49 for a "get out of jail free" card.

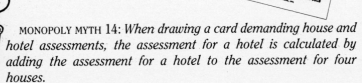

MONOPOLY MYTH 14: *When drawing a card demanding house and hotel assessments, the assessment for a hotel is calculated by adding the assessment for a hotel to the assessment for four houses.*

A hotel is a hotel and a house is a house; a hotel is not the same as four houses and a hotel. To buy a hotel a player must surrender four houses on the lot to the bank. Therefore, a hotel replaces completely four houses. The end result of this is that an assessment for a hotel can be much less costly than an assessment for three or four houses (P4).

MONOPOLY MYTH 15: *It is possible to leave a property unowned after someone lands on it, so that the next player to land on it will have a chance to buy it.*

Some players do not conduct an auction after a player has decided not to buy a piece of property. The rules (H8) clearly require the banker to auction off property after someone has decided not to buy it.

MONOPOLY MYTH 16: *You cannot build a house until all your property is demortgaged.*

Monopoly rule S9 says that property on which a house is to be built must first be unmortgaged. There is no requirement that other owned properties be unmortgaged prior to building a house on any particular lot.

MONOPOLY MYTH 17: *Players may not mortgage properties to get money to buy houses.*
The rules place no restrictions on how you spend the money you get by mortgaging.

MONOPOLY MYTH 18: *The owner of a mortgaged property must demortgage it in order to trade or sell it.*
The rules (S15) specify that it is the player who acquires a mortgaged property who has the obligation either to lift the mortgage immediately or to pay the bank immediately an extra 10 percent interest penalty.

∗ TACTICAL ADVANTAGE 3: Since many players have forgotten about the 10 percent penalty or the immediate unmortgaging rule, knowledgeable players can gain a small advantage by waiting until a deal is finished to bring attention to this rule to the new owner, who would be obligated to pay the 10 percent.

∗ TACTICAL ADVANTAGE 4: When trading for or buying a mortgaged property, try to demand as part of the deal that the current owner first lift the mortgage.

MONOPOLY MYTH 19: *It is permissible to lend money to other players as long as the player who borrows money has to pay interest.*
The last line of the rules (U1) states: "No player may borrow from or lend money to another player." Charging interest does not make a loan legal.
It is easy for skilled players to get around this rule, however. Turn loans into trades or deals. For example, instead of giving someone $100 at 10 percent interest, which is not legal, you could give another player $100 in exchange for an immunity from rent on Baltic Avenue, which is perfectly legal.

Another group of myths reward luck indirectly. These myths bring money into the game faster or less smoothly than in unaltered Monopoly. The pool of money in unaltered Monopoly grows at a predictable, constant rate, and skilled players can take advantage of this fact. Therefore, you should resist the myths that follow.

MONOPOLY MYTH 20: *Place all fines, taxes, and penalties in the center of the board, and any player who lands on Free Parking gets all the money thus collected.*

This is one of the most common Monopoly myths, and even players who know that this is a myth continue to play Monopoly with a Free Parking pot. Playing with a pot puts a larger element of luck into the game, and generally all players wind up with more cash (at least temporarily) than they would have without a pot.

The main effect of adding this rule is to bring more cash into the game, and this will affect the best place and time for players to trade to form monopolies. This rule decreases skilled players' alternatives for monopolies.

MONOPOLY MYTH 21: *Collect double salary ($400) if you land on the Go square.*

The rules (G2) are very clear about this. A player never collects more than $200 salary in a single turn with the exception of when a player passes Go and immediately draws a card that says, "Go to Go." In that case a player does not really collect $400 for a single trip around the board; the player actually made two trips about the board in a single turn.

MONOPOLY MYTH 22: *You do not collect $200 salary for passing Go while traveling to a square as commanded by a Chance card unless the card tells you to do so.*

This myth originated from the fact that some Chance cards say, "If you pass go, collect $200," while other "go to" Chance cards do not.

Actually it makes no difference. Rule G4 states that you collect your salary even if you travel by a card rather than by dice.

HOW TO HANDLE HARMFUL MYTHS

* TACTICAL ADVANTAGE 5: Resist mythical rules that directly reward luck, reduce the number of decisions to be made, or significantly disturb the normal flow of money. Such myths are harmful to skilled players.

It can be difficult to convince your opponents—especially if they have been playing Monopoly for years—that what they believe are rules are really myths.

The first step for avoiding undesired myths is to get a commitment from your partners that the real rules should be followed. A stated commitment ties everyone to the written rules by acknowledging their authority.

* TACTICAL ADVANTAGE 6: Before the first harmful myth arises, obtain a verbal commitment from opposing players early in the game to follow the genuine rules of Monopoly.

The second step is to compromise. You can afford to accept "harmless" myths, those that do not hurt skilled players' chances of winning. In exchange for doing so, make opponents agree to play by the "real rules" when harmful myths are introduced.

* TACTICAL ADVANTAGE 7: Challenge all mythical rules. Concede to play by the myths that you know are not important when doing so forces opponents to concede on the points you really want to win.

The following are a group of unimportant myths that you can use to feed your end of compromises.

MONOPOLY MYTH 23: *Throw a single die to determine which player goes first.*
Most players believe they should use one die instead of two dice for the opening dice throws. The rules actually require dice (not

one die) throughout the entire game, including the opening dice throws.

> **＊ TACTICAL ADVANTAGE 8:** When playing with new opponents, use your knowledge of the words die and dice and their usage in the rules to establish immediately your credentials as a Monopoly rules expert at the very start of the game. This will help you convince your partners that they should play by your interpretation of the rules.

MONOPOLY MYTH 24: *When landing on a Utility, pick up and throw the dice again and pay rent according to how many dots appear.*

This myth is of no consequence, except that doing it correctly (using the initial dice throw; see Utility Title Deed cards) saves a little time. Both methods will on average yield 7. This is another good choice of a challengeable myth to use to establish yourself initially as a Monopoly rules authority.

MONOPOLY MYTH 25: *You may not collect your $200 salary if you forget to ask for it and the next player has already thrown the dice.*

It is the banker's obligation to pay salaries, and players cannot be penalized by the banker's failure to pay promptly.

MONOPOLY MYTH 26: *If the owner of a property fails to ask for rent before the next roll of the dice, the owner has lost that rent forever.*

This is true only when the next roll of the dice is thrown by the next player. It is not true if the person owing the rent has thrown doubles and rolls the dice again.

MONOPOLY MYTH 27: *It is permissible to leave four houses on a lot when a player has built a hotel on the lot.*

A hotel replaces all houses.

MONOPOLY MYTH 28: *When trying to buy a property for which you have insufficient cash, it is permissible to mortgage the property you are buying at the same time that you buy it.*

You must pay for a lot before you may mortgage it.

MONOPOLY MYTH 29: *Upon landing on Income Tax, when adding up the value of assets, use the mortgage value of property if the property is mortgaged.*

Just like the government's laws, Monopoly rules are designed to extract from you greater taxes. Income tax is based on property face value, regardless of any mortgages.

MONOPOLY MYTH 30: *You cannot buy property or be forced to pay rent when sent to a square by a Chance or Community Chest card.*

How you came to land on a particular lot changes neither your options nor your obligations.

MONOPOLY MYTH 31: *You may not buy property until you have passed Go at least once.*

You always have a right to buy unowned property when you have landed on it.

MONOPOLY MYTH 32: *You relinquish the right to a property if you forget to ask for the Title Deed card.*

It is the banker's responsibility to distribute Title Deed cards, and players have no obligation to ask for them.

MONOPOLY MYTH 33: *You cannot charge double rent for landing on a monopolized property, if any of the properties in that color group are mortgaged.*

Rent due depends only on the status of the property itself. The status of all other lots is irrelevant.

MONOPOLY MYTH 34: *If you stay in jail for three turns, you automatically get out of jail free at the end of the third turn.*

If you fail to throw doubles, Monopoly rules show no mercy; you must pay $50 when you leave jail.

MONOPOLY MYTH 35: *You lose the right to another roll of the dice after you've thrown doubles if you land on the Go to Jail square or you draw a card commanding you to go to jail.*

Throwing three doubles consecutively is the only exception to getting another dice throw after rolling doubles.

MONOPOLY MYTH 36: *If you throw doubles while in jail, you immediately leave jail, but you never get to roll the dice a second time.*

The published rules actually provide for no exceptions to the privilege of rolling dice a second time after throwing doubles except in the case in which a player throws three doubles in a row (F5).

The accepted way to handle doubles thrown while in jail is this: If you paid $50 to get out of jail and then throw doubles, you have the privilege of rolling the dice a second time, but if you did not pay $50 first and simply rolled the doubles enabling you to get out of jail free, you lose the right to roll the dice a second time. The idea is that you used up your right to a second throw of the dice in exchange for getting out of jail free.

Certainly, these rules for getting out of jail are complicated, but in this regard Monopoly is like life: generally, getting out of trouble is more difficult than getting into trouble.

4 🚂

Ground Rules to Help You Rule

The Monopoly rules do not cover all potential game situations, so players must agree on ground rules. There is no good reason you should not propose ground rules that are to your advantage.

There are two issues requiring ground rules:

1. When is it permissible to buy houses?
2. Can a player transfer Title Deed restrictions to another player?

BUYING HOUSES

The rules read: "A player may buy and erect . . . at any time as many houses as his judgment and financial standing will allow."

"At any time" could mean that while an opponent is counting out his move, if it looks like he is going to land on your monopoly, you could try to buy more houses before he finished moving his token. This literal interpretation could result in chaos. Furthermore, it is unsportsmanlike and rewards sneakiness.

Assuming that you do not count sneakiness among your Monopoly strengths, it is in your interest to promote a restrictive rule for buying houses.

✱ TACTICAL ADVANTAGE **9:** Propose a restrictive rule about when it is permissible to buy houses.

If you write about this to Parker Brothers, the company will probably tell you that "at any time" means at any time during the buyer's turn. This is a sensible interpretation, and it would be sensible for Parker Brothers to revise the rules slightly to prevent confusion and argument.

Neither do the rules used at official Monopoly tournaments clarify this situation. The published materials for tournaments require house buying to occur "only between turns of other players." This is not, of course, the same as the basic, long rules.

Except for the literal interpretation of "at any time," any reasonable interpretation is acceptable as a ground rule.

You should raise this issue after any opponent gains a developable monopoly or when you want to start negotiating a trade to gain a monopoly, but not before that.

> ∗ **STRATEGIC ADVANTAGE 10:** If possible, do not discuss ground rules for buying houses until you are ready to trade; otherwise, you may prematurely trigger strategic trading by opponents.

TRANSFERRING NONCASH TERMS AND CONDITIONS

Deals and trades between players often include more than hard cash and properties. Immunities from rent, assumption of particular future obligations, and options to buy properties in the future are examples of the creative deals Monopoly players dream up.

Such deals are perfectly legal, even though uninvolved players may howl in protest. Questions arise if, subsequent to such deals, properties change hands. Can players who were originally not a party to such agreements be bound by them?

A specific example may clarify the problem. Suppose you agree to give Player B title to St. James Place. In return you get immunity from rent on all four of Player B's Railroads.

Suppose that later Player B either sells the Railroads to Player C or goes bankrupt. Do you retain your immunity from rent on those railroads? Or must you pay Player C rent each time you land on a railroad? Remember, your immunity "contract" was originally with Player B, not with Player C.

If no ground rule is established, one side will argue endlessly that any agreement between you and Player B should not be binding on Player C. You, on the other hand, will argue that it is not fair to lose immunity on the Railroads, since you gave up a valuable piece of property to gain the immunity in the first place.

The only chance to reach agreement on this potential controversy is to do so *before* the situation arises and to present a persuasive argument why it should be handled in a particular way.

✳ **STRATEGIC ADVANTAGE 11:** At the beginning of any Monopoly game, obtain agreement that deals among players will be handled as if Monopoly properties were "real" real estate.

Almost any deal made between players can be described in terms of traditional, real-world real estate transactions such as mortgages, liens, leaseholds, easements, options, or legacies. If contracts or "deals" between players are considered to be real estate contracts, immunities and other such agreements are transferable to future owners of a property.

Accepting this ground rule accomplishes more than simply avoiding arguments. Handling Monopoly properties according to real estate law can help you to win.

By the time you finish this book, you will know better than your opponents what properties are most to your advantage to acquire. Therefore, it is in your interest to have as much freedom as possible in getting particular properties from other players. It is in your interest to have the freedom to make permanent restrictions on properties, as this improves your ability to close a deal with any particular player.

You should have no difficulty gaining agreement about this if you raise the issue early enough. If any player objects, use the following arguments to get all players to agree.

1. There can be no disputing the fact that Monopoly is a real estate game based substantially on the real world. It follows that the way transfer-of-rights disputes are handled in the real world of real estate transactions should be followed in the game of Monopoly.
2. In the real world, the law permits property owners to put on titles almost any reasonable restriction on the use of prop-

erty, provided that the owner is not insane and does not create a public nuisance. Courts have enforced all manner of title restrictions.

3. For several hundred years, common law has required a purchaser of property to determine whether there are title restrictions that would prohibit the use of the property as intended. Since deals between players are known to all other players, there is no issue in Monopoly about a player not knowing the "prior restrictions on the title." Player C, in the present example, must know that there was a restriction on part of the rent he could get from the Railroads when he acquired them.

4. The rules for the game of Monopoly acknowledge the existence of transferable restrictions on Title Deeds by accepting the existence of mortgages.

5

Dressings for Success

"Dressings" do not mean what you wear, though dress can be part of it. Dressings refer to how you arrange and handle your immediate surroundings and routine tasks.

Why should dressings make a difference toward winning? For the same reasons that sports teams compete better when they play in their own stadium. Monopoly dressings bring about more familiarity, comfort, and relaxation and reduce hassle, distraction, and stress. As a result of all this, good dressings seem to enhance feelings of power and confidence, a psychological edge.

Even when you play an "away game," by exerting some control over dressings you can gain a winning advantage.

MERCHANDISE YOUR GOODS

One reason retailers display what they hope to sell is to let the sight of the items cause shoppers to think, "This is something I should consider buying."

Monopoly also involves selling. Specifically, you sell properties that can form monopolies. The greater the demand for your properties, the more you can extract from opponents when you trade or deal.

It is in your interest, therefore, not only to display Title Deed cards (as the rules require) but to treat them like tiny billboards.

Advertise your properties by positioning your Title Deed cards where they are most easily seen by opponents.

Since players focus their sight on the gameboard on nearly every move, the best attention-getting area is the periphery of the board itself.

⁕ STRATEGIC ADVANTAGE 12: Arrange your Title Deed cards openly at the edge of the board. Do not store cash on top of Title Deed cards.

When you want no one to trade, simply stack the cards on top of each other so only the top one is fully visible.

ADVERTISE YOURSELF

From the game's beginning to its end, Monopoly players' attention shifts back and forth from the gameboard to the bank. The player who sits closest to the bank (who generally serves as the banker) is the one who gets most recognition and is the player spoken to most often. The banker is the player with the most authority. The banker's is the power position, and it brings with it obvious advantages, especially when you are playing in a group that includes people whom you do not know well.

During the game, players adjust their location to make dealing with the banker easier. When it is time to negotiate trades, the banker is likely to have the best negotiating view of all the players. A negotiator must sense what the other side is thinking. In practical terms this means he or she must have a good view of the other side's eyes. People who have studied such things say it is ideal to be at the same level, between 1½ and 7 feet apart.

⁕ STRATEGIC ADVANTAGE 13: Volunteer to be the banker, especially if you are in a game with players you do not know well.

A secondary advantage of being the banker is that you can be more confident that the job of banker is held by an honest person.

∗ STRATEGIC ADVANTAGE 14: If you cannot be the banker, take a seat close to the bank. Volunteer to serve as Title Deed card manager, which carries part of the authority and visibility of the banker.

DISPLAYING CASH

While the rules require Title Deed cards to be openly displayed, there is no such requirement for cash. You can, if you wish, hide some of it so that opponents may come to believe you are poorer than you really are.

The most common reason to hide cash surreptitiously is to convince an opponent that you pose little threat if he or she gives you property by which you gain a monopoly. Poor, you make a better trading partner than someone who could quickly build hotels.

In some circles of players, hiding money is so common that it will simply be assumed that you have more money than you admit to having. You are then almost obliged to hide some of your cash simply to remain on an equal footing.

If you follow the advice in this book, you will be able to see through any significantly large wealth disguises. However, most opponents you face will not have read this book, so it may nevertheless be helpful to you to hide some of your cash from them.

If you decide to hide some cash, do so effectively. Put away only a reasonable amount so as not to arouse suspicion.

Monopoly money is easy to put away or to retrieve without being detected, because when any player rolls the dice, all eyes follow the player's token as the squares are counted.

With that distraction, there are any number of places money can be conveniently hidden: under the board, under Title Deed cards, under one's thigh, inside of smoking materials, under plates or inside empty cups, or in a sleeve or pocket.

Should you be so clumsy as to be detected while putting aside some of your cash, humor is probably the best response ("I was making sure no one would steal it from me").

You do not want to let yourself be exposed as a cash hider because given a choice between trading with a player whose cash is all on the table and one who is suspected of having some stashed away, a player will choose to trade with the player displaying the cash, if all else is equal. The cash hider presents an uncertainty. People prefer certainty to uncertainty, especially when, as in Monopoly, there is a surplus of uncertainty from the beginning.

✳ STRATEGIC ADVANTAGE 15: Do not hide cash in a way or to such an extent that you arouse suspicion. Do not openly hide cash, as this builds uncertainty in potential trade partners.

The question arises what to do if you want to trade with a player who you know has cash hidden away but who claims not to have any more cash to include as part of the trade. You must stick to your demand for the amount of money you want and give your trading partner time to raise it. You might hint that you are certain that the player could come up with the necessary cash quickly.

✳ STRATEGIC ADVANTAGE 16: Give opponents who have money hidden some time to raise the cash you demand, so that they can retrieve their cash inconspicuously.

ESTABLISH A STYLE AND STAY WITH IT

You will get more free landings if you establish and maintain a consistent style of rolling the dice and counting the squares. Many players unconsciously change their style when they become concerned about where they will land. Through their change of style they unwittingly send a signal to opponents that something is afoot. As a result, all players pay special attention.

Maintaining a uniform style has another advantage. When you want an opponent to keep in mind where your token is located, you can change your style, and he will notice where on the board you have landed.

✳ TACTICAL ADVANTAGE 10: Establish a dice-rolling and token-moving style so that your token's position gets as little or as much attention as you prefer.

AVOID LOST RENTS

You do not want to miss opponents' landings on your property. The U.S. version of Monopoly makes reading the name of property on the opposite side of the board somewhat challenging: you must read a property's name upside down. (Foreign-language versions of Monopoly eliminate this problem by featuring the property name twice in each square, once right side up and once upside down.)

Identifying squares is no problem for people who are very familiar with the board or who have excellent eyesight. In the absence of both, you must simply ask, "What is that square?" This advice may seem too obvious to mention, but to legions of squinting players it is not.

DO NOT HELP OPPONENTS REMEMBER CARDS

In a game of typical length, all Chance and Community Chest cards are used at least once. Do not help opponents remember the order in which they appeared.

Develop a consistent style of reading cards. Read them aloud word for word, but do not display them. People remember better what they see than what they hear. Word-for-word reading will convince opponents you are not inventing a favorable card. At the same time, if you alone see the card, you will have an advantage in remembering it.

＊TACTICAL ADVANTAGE 11: Share Chance and Community Chest cards with your opponents verbally, not visually.

GET A HELICOPTER'S VIEW

Before you can negotiate successfully, you must figure out what it is you want. In Monopoly this requires that you see who owns what and what will be the effect of particular changes in ownership. If blessed with a genius-class brain, you can do this in the solitude of your own mind. Otherwise, it is helpful to see all players' properties at one time.

This is most easily achieved by taking a stretch. Stand up behind your seat so that you can see everyone's properties at about the same time.

* **STRATEGIC ADVANTAGE 17:** When you have to do some serious thinking about various trade alternatives, get a helicopter's view by taking a stretch.

TIME-OF-GAME CLOCK

In Monopoly a time-of-the-game clock is as helpful as a clock is to daily life. You cannot use an ordinary clock to tell the time of the game because different groups of players play at different speeds.

To win Monopoly it helps always to know how close the game is to having had about 40 passes of Go, a critical point strategically for a number of reasons detailed later.

If you put a $1 bill under your cash pile each time a player passes Go, you would always know how close you were to Monopoly's most important decision point by simply counting your bottom $1 bills.

* **STRATEGIC ADVANTAGE 18:** Keep a game clock: each time any player passes Go, put a $1 bill in a certain place in your cash holdings.

PART TWO

BELOW THE SURFACE
OF MONOPOLY

Every game of Monopoly is different because there are infinite combinations of possible events. However, each game is long enough to give possible events repeated chances to happen, which means that the laws of probability govern the action.

The laws of probability cause certain patterns of events to form in almost every game, and if you know what they are, you can use these patterns to help you win.

The problem is that you cannot rely on your memory to find all the usual patterns of events in Monopoly. Too many things happen from game to game for the brain to sort out the typical from the strange.

For example, some players believe that certain natural monopolies are more rare than others. To someone who had never been in a game in which the Marvin Gardens monopoly formed naturally, it would seem reasonable to conclude that Marvin Gardens is more difficult to monopolize than other three-lot monopolies. But if you could study data from thousands of games, you could clearly see that all natural three-lot monopolies form equally often.

The chapters in Part Two show tabulations of data from thousands of games to let you see useful trends and landmark events that take place in virtually every game.

UNLOCKING THE GAME'S SECRETS WITH COMPUTERIZED SIMULATIONS

Most of the data in the charts and graphs in the remainder of this book are based on a computer's memory. As computers have no difficulty "remembering" almost infinite detail, the source of the advice you read in this book is superior to personal recollections and subjective opinions.

Not only did a computer record the events, but a computer

played the games. (It would have taken a group of human players over 53 years of continuous, round-the-clock play to complete the 187,000 games whose results are reported in this book.)

Since these computer-played games are the basis for most of this book's content, you may be interested in how these games were played.

A computer was programmed to follow all the rules of Monopoly, to roll dice, to impose rents and taxes, to dispense Chance and Community Chest cards, and so on. An artificial intelligence was programmed into the computer to enable it to make playing decisions on behalf of any number of imaginary players.

Each imaginary player was programmed to have absolutely equal "playing ability"; that is, each imaginary player considered the same factors and used identical logic when making decisions. Such equality among players does not exist in games among real human players; nevertheless, perfect equality is an advantage for learning how to win Monopoly.

First, when one perfectly equal imaginary player was found to win more than his share of games, it could not have been due to a human variable such as personality or intelligence. Another advantage was that using computer-controlled imaginary players eliminated the effects of luck by playing every experimental game hundreds or thousands of times and by using certain statistical controls. Controlling all outside influences in this way made it possible to isolate the causal factor whenever one imaginary player won more than his share of a group of similar games.

In some sets of these games, all players were programmed to follow identical guidelines when making decisions, leaving only one factor to explain a particular player's superior winning record: wealth (property and cash). Such experimental games made it possible to isolate and study the effect of particular game situations on players' ability to win.

In other games one imaginary player was programmed to make a particular decision differently from other imaginary players, with all other factors held equal. Won-lost records thus provided a way to determine objectively the best decisions to win Monopoly and the strategies and tactics humans who want to win should adopt.

Most of the data in the remainder of this book, as well as most of the tactical and strategic advantages, are based on one of these two types of experimental games.

6

The Secret Value of Properties

Virtually every Monopoly player has at least one favorite property and possibly some favorite monopolies too. Some players also have strong beliefs that certain properties are dogs—lots that are usually not worth what they cost.

WHY PROPERTY VALUES IN MONOPOLY REMAIN SECRET

Which properties reward their owners and which pull the owner into defeat are important questions, and some writers about Monopoly have tried in the past to supply answers. They have relied on what Monopoly players generally rely on when selecting favorites: personal experience while owning particular lots.

There are problems with relying on personal experience and memory to analyze something variable like Monopoly. One problem is that human memory is limited. Another is that Monopoly requires each player in each game to make a number of decisions, causing the connection between any one decision (such as to buy or not to buy a property) and the end result (winning or losing) to become fuzzy.

Consequently, much of what has in the past been written about how to distinguish a valuable Monopoly property from a poor one is simply inaccurate. The true worth of individual Monopoly properties has largely remained secret.

To determine the real value of properties it is necessary to combine accurate, hard data from many games with a technique commonly used in business and banking called return-on-investment analysis. It is useful to follow the analysis rather than to go directly to the results.

ANALYZING THE SECRET VALUES OF PROPERTIES

The main value of any property in Monopoly is that it can earn the owner rental income. Rental income depends on how often opposing players land on a piece of property as well as on the basic rental rate. Assuming that one property is as likely to be landed on as any other property is the first common mistake.

The second error is to assume that the rent collectible from a property is proportional to the price of the property.

To see how one Monopoly property compares with another it is necessary to understand the concept of return on investment (ROI). This concept is similar to the interest paid on bank savings accounts.

The basic return on investment for Monopoly properties can be calculated with the assumption that every property will be landed on one time by a rent-paying opponent. The return on investment for Virginia Avenue, therefore, is $12 rent divided by $160 property cost, or 7.5 percent.

Figure 6.1 is a graph of the basic return on investment for all properties. If you study the table, you will note that except for Railroads and Utilities, there is a pattern to the rents and ROIs. As you go around the board the rents, of course, increase, but the returns on investment increase even faster. This means that the more expensive properties in Monopoly are more valuable in two ways: they pay more rent, and the returns on your invested money are higher.

* **TACTICAL ADVANTAGE 12:** Buy properties with the idea that higher-priced properties are a bargain. The higher purchase prices are compensated by yet greater ROIs; that is, the rents of higher-priced properties go up faster than the lot prices.

FIGURE 6.1

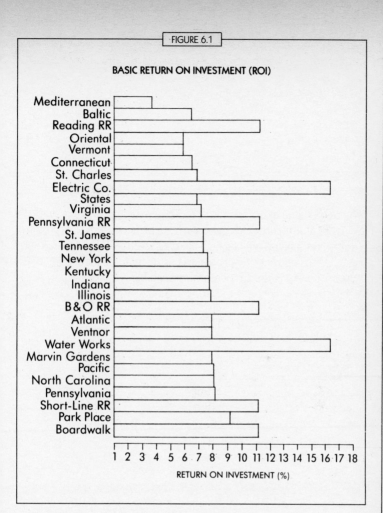

BASIC RETURN ON INVESTMENT (ROI)

RETURN ON INVESTMENT (%)

The cheap Monopoly properties are too expensive, and the expensive properties are a bargain.

LANDING ON OWNABLE LOTS

Because Jail causes players to retrace their steps over part of the board and because "go to" cards cause players to skip over portions

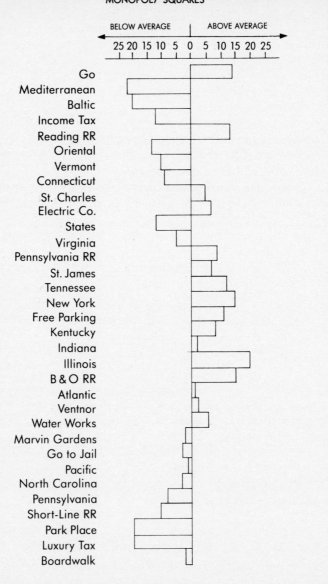

FIGURE 6.2

RELATIVE LANDING FREQUENCIES OF SELECTED MONOPOLY SQUARES

BELOW AVERAGE | ABOVE AVERAGE

25 20 15 10 5 0 5 10 15 20 25

Go
Mediterranean
Baltic
Income Tax
Reading RR
Oriental
Vermont
Connecticut
St. Charles
Electric Co.
States
Virginia
Pennsylvania RR
St. James
Tennessee
New York
Free Parking
Kentucky
Indiana
Illinois
B & O RR
Atlantic
Ventnor
Water Works
Marvin Gardens
Go to Jail
Pacific
North Carolina
Pennsylvania
Short-Line RR
Park Place
Luxury Tax
Boardwalk

of the board, landings on properties on some parts of the board are likely to be more frequent than on others.

The zero line in Figure 6.2 represents the average landing frequency for all ownable properties on the board. The distance that the bars are above or below the zero line correspond to how far above or below average the landing frequency on a property truly is. For example, Boardwalk is landed on 2 percent less frequently than the average ownable property, and Indiana Avenue is landed on 2 percent more often than the average ownable property.

It is fortunate that the landing frequencies form a rather regular pattern because it would be very difficult to remember the landing frequencies of so many properties. But since they do form a regular pattern, it is necessary only to remember the basic pattern and to take notice of the few exceptions to it.

Judging how often players land on a particular lot could hardly be more simple: landing frequency is proportional to the lot's closeness to the Free Parking square.

> ✳ **TACTICAL ADVANTAGE 13:** When judging the value of a property, consider its closeness to Free Parking as an indication how many times players will land on it.

The first exception to the general pattern is Reading Railroad, which one might expect to be a below-average property; instead, players land on it 13 percent more often than average. The reason is that there are a number of cards commanding players to Reading.

The next exception is Electric Company, which gains its above-average status from two factors: a "Go to the nearest Utility" Chance card and catching players throwing doubles as they come out of jail.

St. Charles Place is a minor exception in that you would expect it to be an average property but it is above average. Boardwalk is a below-average property, but it is not as far below average as would be expected from the general pattern. St. Charles and Boardwalk

FIGURE 6.3

BEST AND WORST PROPERTIES IN TERMS OF LANDING FREQUENCY

During Entire Games		When Players Stay in Jail up to Three Turns	
Best	Percent of Average	Best	Percent of Average
Illinois	120	Illinois	120
B&O RR	115	B&O RR	115
New York	115	Tennessee	115
Reading RR	113	Reading RR	113
Tennessee	112	New York	112
Pennsylvania RR	109	Electric Co.	111
Kentucky	108	St. James	110
St. James	107	Pennsylvania RR	106
Worst		Worst	
Mediterranean	78	Mediterranean	76
Park Place	80	Park Place	81
Baltic	80	Baltic	83
Oriental	87	Oriental	89
Short Line RR	89	Short Line RR	89
Vermont	90	Connecticut	89
Connecticut	91	Pennsylvania	91
Pennsylvania	92	Vermont	92

The properties downstream of jail in even numbers gain in landing frequency when players stay in jail trying to get out of jail free. The worst properties are virtually unaffected by players' jail-stay policy.

each benefit from a "go to" Chance card. See Figure 6.3 for a summary of the best and worst properties in terms of landing frequency.

LANDING FREQUENCY DISTRIBUTION AND STAYING IN JAIL

The landing distribution just described applies when players make intelligent choices about how long to stay in jail. If players never choose to leave jail early, the properties that are within a doubles' throw of the jail square are landed on relatively more often. The overall landing pattern is unchanged by the jail-stay decision that players make, but Electric Company, Virginia, St. James, and Tennessee become stronger properties because of their position in relation to jail. Details are shown in Figure 6.3.

"REAL" RETURNS ON INVESTMENTS

To determine the real, secret values of individual properties, it is necessary to adjust upward the rents for properties that are landed on more frequently than average and to adjust downward the rents earned by properties that are landed on less frequently than the average.

Figure 6.4 deserves some study, because the adjusted ROIs represent the real ROIs, whereas the original, unadjusted ROIs correspond to what many Monopoly players think (mistakenly) are the real value of those properties. All of the real, adjusted ROIs are higher than the unadjusted ROIs for the properties close to Free Parking.

> * TACTICAL ADVANTAGE 14: When trading for rental properties, trade for properties in the neighborhood of Free Parking, because those properties are most likely to be undervalued by opponents.

Away from Free Parking, all properties are less valuable than they appear; that is, all have real, adjusted ROIs smaller than their actual ROIs, with these exceptions:

1. Almost all the Railroads and Utilities have higher real, adjusted ROIs than they originally appeared to have. Only Short-Line Railroad has a lower real ROI.
2. St. Charles Place has a slightly higher adjusted real ROI than the original, perceived ROI because of the "Go to St. Charles" Chance card.

THE CASH COWS

The real world of business recognizes a certain type of company by the expression "cash cow." Cash cows are companies that have

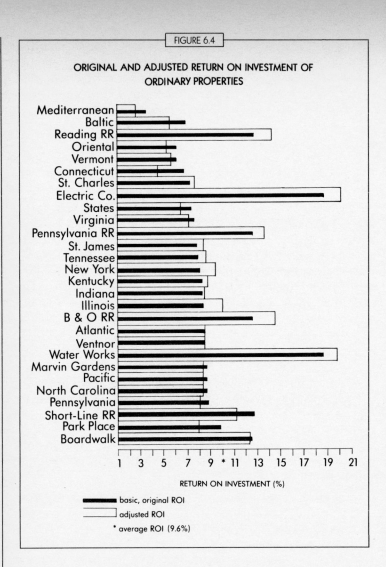

FIGURE 6.4

ORIGINAL AND ADJUSTED RETURN ON INVESTMENT OF ORDINARY PROPERTIES

Mediterranean
Baltic
Reading RR
Oriental
Vermont
Connecticut
St. Charles
Electric Co.
States
Virginia
Pennsylvania RR
St. James
Tennessee
New York
Kentucky
Indiana
Illinois
B & O RR
Atlantic
Ventnor
Water Works
Marvin Gardens
Pacific
North Carolina
Pennsylvania
Short-Line RR
Park Place
Boardwalk

1 3 5 7 9 * 11 13 15 17 19 21

RETURN ON INVESTMENT (%)

— basic, original ROI
☐ adjusted ROI
* average ROI (9.6%)

been in business for a long time and are involved with products that do not change much. Owners of cash cows do not have to reinvest much of their profits to remain in business.

The cash cows in Monopoly are the Railroads and the Utilities. Among the players who do not realize the value of cash cows are

persons who have written about Monopoly. A writer from England
wrote about Railroads and Utilities this way: "Only buy them if you
can really afford them. [They] may be regarded as luxuries until
the game gets properly under way." A book about Monopoly published in the United States contained a section titled "The Utilities
Folly." The author said, "Utilities are generally the worst investments on the board."

It is wonderful that these writers (and Monopoly players in general) think of Railroads and Utilities as almost worthless properties,
because that makes it much easier for you to get them.

You may have noticed that most of the properties that have
above-average ROIs are, in fact, the Railroads and the Utilities.
Furthermore, the superiority of cash cows over other properties
widens when the ROIs are adjusted for landing frequency because
they all (with the exception of Short-Line Railroad) have higher-
than-average landing frequencies. When it comes to making
money from individual properties, there is no better way than to
collect Railroads and Utilities.

The relative superiority of the cash cows grows again when you
consider that they can be assembled into minor monopolies. When
monopolized into four Railroads or into three Railroads plus both
Utilities, the cash cows' ROIs become so high that the owner gains
a major winning advantage: a cash cow monopoly will extract from
every opponent most of the cash each earns from circling the
board!

Like most Monopoly players, you may have a poor opinion of
the Utilities and Railroads because you cannot develop them into
killer monopolies. It is true that cash cows cannot bankrupt opponents directly. However, to make any killer monopoly a killer
you need cash, and there is no better way to earn cash than
through the Railroads and the Utilities.

If your neighborhood bank offered, say, 20 percent interest on
your money but limited you to a $1000 maximum balance, you
would be silly not to put some of your money in that bank just
because you had more than $1000 to put away. The sensible thing
to do would be to put the maximum amount of money in the 20
percent account and to put the rest of your money someplace else.

The advantage to investing in the Railroads and Utilities in Monopoly is similar. The return on your investment is very high, but
you are limited as to the amount of your investment.

The sensible thing to do with cash cows is to do exactly what real-world, modern-day conglomerates do: they use cash cows to generate excess cash that can be reinvested in other companies with greater growth potential.

Invest the small amount of money it takes to get the cash cows, and use the cash that they generate to build up the cash necessary to build your developable monopolies and make them more powerful.

It turns out that your ability to raise cash to build up the healthy cash balances necessary to buy houses and hotels depends more on how many Utilities and Railroads you own than on any other single factor in the game of Monopoly. The value of Utilities and Railroads is truly one of the best-kept secrets in Monopoly.

* TACTICAL ADVANTAGE 15: Evaluate Utilities and Railroads as cash generators and not as killer monopolies. Trade for Utilities and Railroads early in the game to earn cash for your later monopoly.

7 🚂

The Secret Value of Monopolies

Monopolies are valuable because they bring in far more rental income than individual lots.

There are two reasons why monopolies bring in more money. First, monopolies allow a much greater investment, which besides presenting a benefit also presents problems. It costs about four times as much to put hotels on a lot than it does to buy the lot alone. Second, the return on investment for monopolies exceeds the return on investment for ordinary properties. In this book properties that are not monopolized are called ordinary properties. When an ordinary property is monopolized and fully developed— that is, when it gains a hotel—rents increase about 38 times.

RANKING THE MONOPOLIES

The usual way players rank the monopolies is according to their potential rents or costs. The expensive monopolies are often called heavy monopolies because they usually require a slow, long-term effort to develop, after which they can deliver a crushing blow to opponents. The inexpensive monopolies are called the light monopolies because building hotels on them is relatively painless and fast.

Figure 7.1 shows the unadjusted rents from all developable monopolies. In effect this graph shows what players generally *believe* are the relative values of the various monopolies.

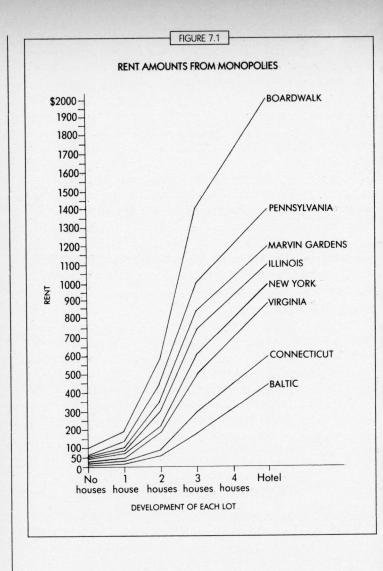

FIGURE 7.1

RENT AMOUNTS FROM MONOPOLIES

RENT

BOARDWALK
PENNSYLVANIA
MARVIN GARDENS
ILLINOIS
NEW YORK
VIRGINIA
CONNECTICUT
BALTIC

No houses / 1 house / 2 houses / 3 houses / 4 houses / Hotel

DEVELOPMENT OF EACH LOT

LANDING ON MONOPOLIES

To get a true idea of the comparative strength of the various monopolies, it is necessary to factor into the rents the relative frequency with which players land on them, as was done previously for ordinary properties. Figure 7.2 shows the results of thousands of games in which the frequency of landing on each of the monopolies was measured.

As was found with the ordinary properties, the most frequently landed-on monopolies are those closest to Free Parking: New York and Illinois. Monopolies suffer a step-by-step decline in landings as their distance from Free Parking increases.

One significance of this is that the rental income of an owner of a monopoly close to Go is less steady than that enjoyed by an owner of a monopoly that has a higher landing frequency. A steady income can be a crucial advantage for a player struggling to survive opponents' monopolies and struggling simultaneously to develop his or her own monopoly.

＊STRATEGIC ADVANTAGE 19: Do not undervalue monopolies close to Free Parking, as many players are liable to do. Such

---

FIGURE 7.2

PROBABILITY OF LANDING ON ANY SQUARE OF A GIVEN MONOPOLY DURING ONE CIRCUIT OF THE BOARD

Monopoly	Landing Frequency	
	Percent	Ratio (approximate)
Baltic	24.6	¼
Connecticut	42.4	½
Virginia	46.0	½
New York	52.4	½
Illinois	52.0	½
Marvin Gardens	47.0	½
Pennsylvania	46.4	½
Boardwalk	28.3	¼
Railroads (4)	66.8	⅔
Utilities (2)	33.0	⅓
Averages		
Developable monopolies	43.4	
Nondevelopable monopolies	49.9	
All monopolies	43.8	

monopolies bring advantages from both the steadiness of the rents and from higher-than-apparent rents.

Both two-lot monopolies, Baltic and Boardwalk, have a two-sided handicap: they are farthest away from Free Parking, and they each have one less lot than the other developable monopolies.

∗ **STRATEGIC ADVANTAGE 20:** Do not overvalue Baltic or Boardwalk due to a belief they are landed on two-thirds as often as are the three-lot monopolies. Actually, players land on Baltic or Boardwalk only about half as often as they land on three-lot monopolies.

TAKE NOTE OF APPROXIMATE LANDING FREQUENCIES

Knowing the frequency with which players land on a particular monopoly is useful for effectively buying houses, trading for monopolies, estimating the value of immunities, and other important tasks in Monopoly as explained later. It is not, however, necessary to memorize all the various landing frequencies. Simply take a close look at the approximate landing frequency ratios in Figure 7.2; they are easy to remember.

∗ **TACTICAL ADVANTAGE 16:** Note that the landing frequencies on any monopoly—including nondevelopable monopolies—can be approximated by a fraction expressed in quarters, thirds, or halves.

THE REAL VALUE OF MONOPOLIES

As was done for ordinary properties, the rents of monopolies can be adjusted according to how often players land on each monopoly. Doing so reveals each monopoly's real or "secret" value. Monopoly owners will on average collect from each opponent during each circuit of the board the amounts of rents shown in Figure 7.3.

The most surprising fact Figure 7.3 reveals is that you cannot count on the price of a monopoly to tell you how much rent you are likely to collect. Boardwalk earns less rent than either the New York, Illinois, or Marvin Gardens monopoly. The Illinois monopoly earns more rent than the more expensive Marvin Gardens monop-

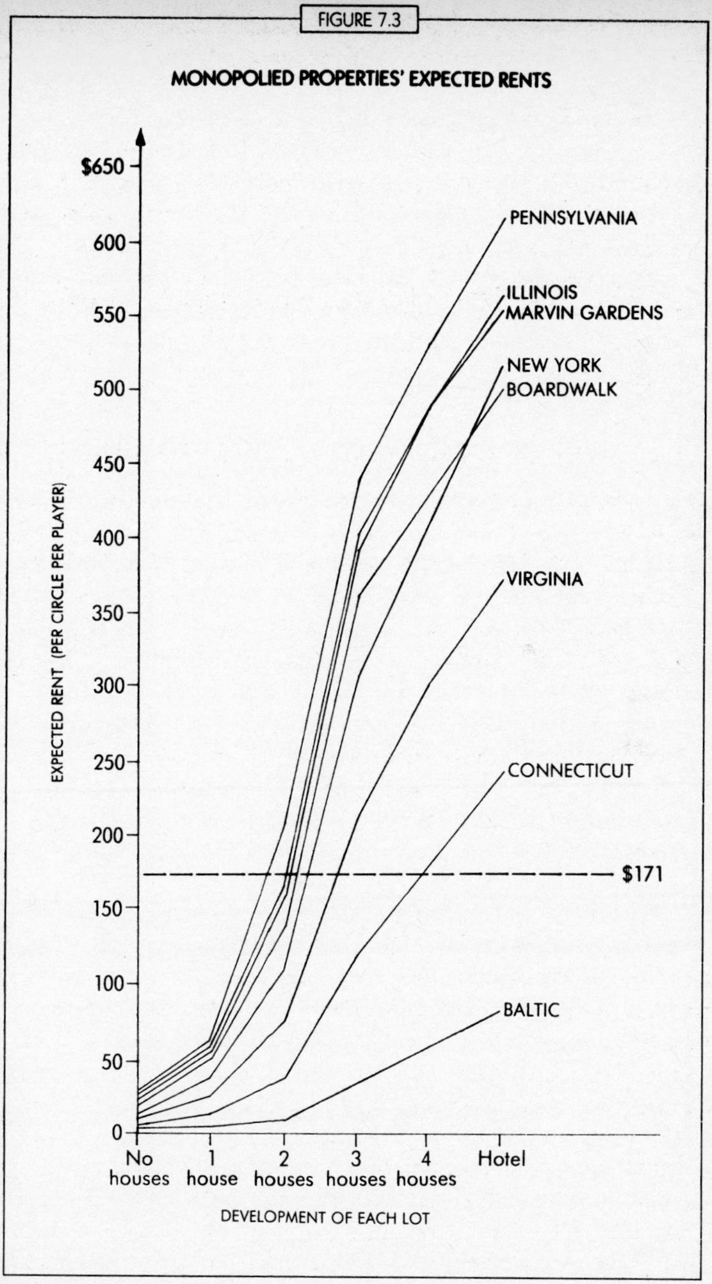
FIGURE 7.3
MONOPOLIED PROPERTIES' EXPECTED RENTS
EXPECTED RENT (PER CIRCLE PER PLAYER)
$650
600
550
500
450
400
350
300
250
200
150
100
50
0
PENNSYLVANIA
ILLINOIS
MARVIN GARDENS
NEW YORK
BOARDWALK
VIRGINIA
CONNECTICUT
BALTIC
$171
No houses
1 house
2 houses
3 houses
4 houses
Hotel
DEVELOPMENT OF EACH LOT

oly. The New York monopoly outearns the Boardwalk monopoly, even though houses on the New York monopoly cost half as much as those on Boardwalk.

Note how little difference there is among the expected rents of any of the five most expensive monopolies. These five heavier monopolies form an upper tier of monopolies that differ from one another by only a relatively small amount.

> ✳ STRATEGIC ADVANTAGE 21: Keep in mind that the similarities in expected rents among the five upper-tier monopolies make it difficult for an upper-tier monopoly owner to defeat with certainty another player owning an upper-tier monopoly, if all else is equal.

There is more difference between the Virginia and Connecticut monopolies than there is between all of the upper-tier monopolies together.

Figure 7.3 shows several ways in which you can take advantage of the fact that the real values of certain monopolies are not what they appear to be.

> ✳ STRATEGIC ADVANTAGE 22: Take advantage of the fact that most players believe that the Boardwalk monopoly is more valuable than the New York monopoly.

> ✳ STRATEGIC ADVANTAGE 23: Take advantage of the fact that most players believe that the Marvin Gardens monopoly is more valuable than the Illinois monopoly.

> ✳ STRATEGIC ADVANTAGE 24: Take advantage of the fact that most players believe that the Illinois and Marvin Gardens monopolies are significantly more lucrative than the New York monopoly, even though the difference is nominal.

WHAT IS THE BEST MONOPOLY?

Obviously, no monopoly is perfect for all game situations; however, one monopoly stands out as being the most versatile: the New York monopoly.

The houses for the New York monopoly are cheap enough that they can be developed almost as fast as the lighter monopolies. At the same time, the expected rents from this monopoly ranks New York in the upper tier.

✻ **STRATEGIC ADVANTAGE 25:** When in doubt about the best monopoly for you in a particular game, aim to get the New York monopoly.

8

Patterns and Milestones

Suppose that someone starting at Go advanced a marker one square each time any player passed Go to collect a salary. By the time the marker reached the Boardwalk monopoly, a number of milestone events would have probably occurred.

THE ACQUISITION PERIOD

During the time the marker passes from Go to Vermont (8 passes of Go), 20 of the 28 properties will typically have been sold. Hardly ever will you encounter a player who does not buy every property he or she can during this 20-minute period.

By the time the marker reaches New York Avenue (19 passes of Go), the average player (no matter how many players are in the game) will have accumulated $1500 in liquid assets (cash plus the mortgage value of all owned properties). By this time, most players know if they have a chance for a natural monopoly or not.

When the marker reaches B&O Railroad (25 passes of Go), the last unsold property will have been sold. At the speed of a casual players' game, it takes about an hour to reach this point. The sale of the last property serves as a signal to all players without monopolies to switch their attention from buying properties to trading for monopolies.

MONOPOLY'S CRUCIAL MILESTONE

Assuming that no one has gained a killer monopoly, the marker will eventually reach Luxury Tax (38 passes of Go). Even if you had not been keeping track of the time by means of a "game clock," at this point alarms ring to remind all how far the game has progressed.

"Alarms"

The first "alarm" is that Chance and Community Chest cards appear for a second showing. Second, the average cash balance players hold again stands at $1500, just as when the game started. (This holds true regardless of the number of players in the game.)

The importance of this milestone and of these alarms will be detailed later. You will see that sometimes you will not want the game to reach this milestone without having traded for a monopoly. Therefore, it is useful to know how long you have before these alarms sound. This is the major reason why a time-of-game clock as suggested earlier (Strategic Advantage 18, Chapter 5) helps you win.

> *** STRATEGIC ADVANTAGE 26:** Use a time-of-game clock to monitor how close the players are to having had passed Go 38 times.

If players trade to form killer monopolies before the alarms signal 38 Go passes, the $1500 average cash balance level will not be reached, because most of the cash players hold will go to the bank to pay for houses.

There is, of course, no set time for trading to take place, though usually it is after all properties have been sold. There is, however, a predictable pattern to the trading of properties.

THE MONOPOLY CHAIN REACTION

Since killer monopolies are usually formed through trades, killer monopolies are usually born in pairs—one to each of two players. Such monopolies are, of course, born at the same point in time.

The sudden emergence of the first two killer monopolies into the game quickly spurs all thinking players without such monopolies to reevaluate their positions. These players soon conclude that they also must have their own killer monopoly. The first major trade is thus quickly followed by additional trades or deals creating more monopolies.

Typically, therefore, monopolies form in chain-reaction fashion, two at a time. Monopolies are usually born in pairs because most players are unwilling to give an opponent a monopoly-forming property unless they receive one in return.

An important consequence of the typical monopoly formation sequence is that the most important decisions of the game for each player are made close together in time.

Players who do not think ahead about their strategy are liable to make their most important decision without much time for analysis.

⁎ **STRATEGIC ADVANTAGE 27:** Take advantage of the lack of time for thoughtful analysis due to the chain-reaction sequence of monopoly trading by planning your trades well in advance.

The two-by-two sequence of monopoly formation leads to a major peril when there are an odd number of players in the game. One player is liable to be left without any opponent with a motivation to deal or trade with that player. The win rate for such a player is low.

⁎ **STRATEGIC ADVANTAGE 28:** Be extra aggressive in promoting deals and be extra receptive to deals proposed to you when you are in a game with an odd number of players. You must avoid being the last and only player without a monopoly.

When the game reaches the point that the trading chain reaction takes place, skill definitely supplants luck in importance.

BANKRUPTCY

Houses first appear during or immediately after the Monopoly chain reaction. It may seem logical to treat bankruptcy as a separate stage of the game after houses and hotels. But in fact most players go bankrupt while opponents are still struggling to build hotels. Only when the Monopoly chain reaction occurs extraordinarily late in the game do numerous players, all owning hotels, survive together for an appreciable length of time.

This is contrary to what you will see when a Monopoly game is depicted in a movie or on a TV show. The players invariably have a board full of houses and hotels, though no one has gone bankrupt. To win Monopoly it pays to be more in tune with the reality of the game than film directors seem to be!

THE 6-5-4 PATTERN

The events covered so far describe the overall patterns of a typical Monopoly game. It is also useful to have an insight into what happens during a typical circuit of the board. You can expect to follow a 6-5-4 pattern. It takes five turns on average to make one complete circuit of the board. During those five turns you can expect to move your token six times. The extra move comes from doubles or "go to" cards. During those six moves you can expect to land on properties four times.

How often during these four landings you will have to pay rent depends on what fraction of the 28 properties you own and what fraction opponents own. If you own, for example, half the properties, you will on average pay rent twice during a circuit. If you own a quarter of the properties, you will pay rent three times during a typical circuit, assuming that nothing is mortgaged.

9 🚂

Managing Cash Flow

Monopoly provides an interesting camouflage to keep all players—at least temporarily—looking and feeling good. For much of the game, soon-to-be losers seem to be as prosperous as the player destined to win.

Monopoly's camouflage is cash flow. Every player enjoys a positive cash flow most of the time.

Cash flow is simply the surplus of cash income over cash expenses. Cash expenses include ordinary rents that must be paid, income tax, luxury tax, and penalties from Chance and Community Chest but does not include cash spent to buy property. Purchases of property are investments, not expenses. Cash income comes from salary, rewards from Chance and Community Chest, and rent paid by opponents.

Through most of the game, having enough cash is a simple matter—you simply take what the bank gives you in the form of salary and card awards. The bank tends to hand out cash rather evenly among all players, differences being due almost entirely to luck. Figures 9.1 and 9.2 show how fast fresh, new money from the bank enters the game and how it is divided among the players. Note that rents paid or collected bring no additional money into the game. Rents simply redistribute already circulating money.

＊TACTICAL ADVANTAGE 17: Use $171 as the best estimate of how much net cash you will get from the bank during a circuit of the board.

FIGURE 9.1

NET CASH FLOW PER CIRCUIT PER PLAYER

Sources of Cash

Salaries	$200	92%
Net income from Chance and Community Chest	18	8%
Net cash income	$218	100%

Uses of Cash

Income tax	$28.00	60%
Luxury tax	9.50	20%
Jail fines	9.50	20%
Cash outflow	$47.00	100%

Net cash gain per player per circuit = $218 − 47 = $171

This table shows cash transactions that add or subtract wealth to the game. In an average circuit, a player will gain $171 in cash. Players also gain or lose cash according to how rents are divided among players. Rents are not included in the chart because rent income and rent expenses vary from player to player and from game to game.

FIGURE 9.2

NET CASH FLOW PER HOUR OF PLAY
(150 MOVES, 26 PASSES OF GO)

Number of players	8	7	6	5	4	3	2
Wealth gain per player	$500	$571	$667	$800	$1000	$1333	$2000
Wealth gain for all players	$4000	$4000	$4000	$4000	$4000	$4000	$4000

Although the flow of wealth into the Monopoly is constant, this wealth must be shared. The dollar amounts shown exclude rent payments among players.

* TACTICAL ADVANTAGE 18: Use your knowledge that $4000 enters the game every hour along with the "Monopoly game clock" to estimate players' total assets.

Cash flow is an effective camouflage because the bank pumps cash into the game fast enough to make up all cash expenses, including deficits any player may have from needing to pay more to opponents for ordinary rent than he or she collects in rent. (The worst ordinary rent deficit any player ever suffers is $80 per circuit of the board.) Thus in the absence of monopolies, all players grow steadily richer. Playing long enough in a game without monopolies enables any Monopoly player eventually to become a millionaire!

To gain more than an even share of the total wealth in a game, it is necessary to force it out of the hands of opponents through rents. Think back to your winning Monopoly games. You will remember that you collected much cash from opposing players, while what you collected from the bank was ordinary. And most of what you took from opponents undoubtedly came from rents on developed monopolized properties after the monopoly chain reaction.

GOOD CASH FLOW MANAGEMENT

Therefore, managing cash flow is not a concern in Monopoly—except during and immediately after the monopoly chain reaction. The monopoly chain reaction, however, happens to be the most critical part of the game, if you want to win.

Managing cash flow means getting enough cash to build enough houses after the monopoly chain reaction to extract from opponents huge monopoly rents.

A PROFILE OF CASH AND WEALTH DURING TYPICAL GAMES

The total assets, liquid assets, and cash balances at all stages of Monopoly games with various numbers of players are displayed in Figure 9.3. Note that total assets increase steadily, while liquid assets and cash balances dip in the early part of the game due to the buying of properties. You can relate these events to the stages and milestones described in Chapter 8.

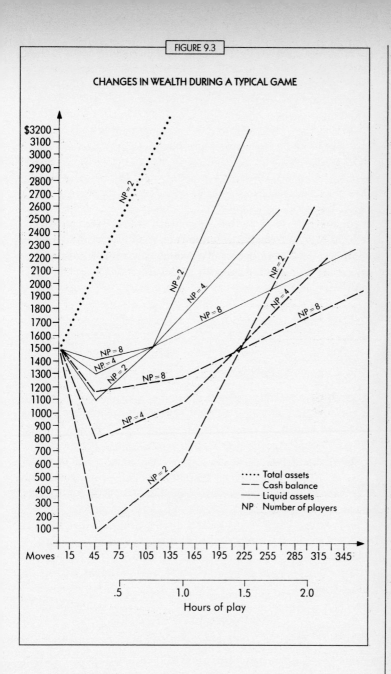

FIGURE 9.3

CHANGES IN WEALTH DURING A TYPICAL GAME

$3200
3100
3000
2900
2800
2700
2600
2500
2400
2300
2200
2100
2000
1900
1800
1700
1600
1500
1400
1300
1200
1100
1000
900
800
700
600
500
400
300
200
100

NP = 2
NP = 2
NP = 4
NP = 8
NP = 8
NP = 4
NP = 2
NP = 8
NP = 4
NP = 2
NP = 4
NP = 8
NP = 2

Moves   15   45   75   105   135   165   195   225   255   285   315   345

.5   1.0   1.5   2.0
Hours of play

······ Total assets
— — — Cash balance
——— Liquid assets
NP   Number of players

Total assets are the face value of owned properties plus cash on hand. Total assets are important only when calculating income tax liability or when playing one of the Monopoly short games. Cash balances are simply the amount of paper money a player has in hand.

Note in Figure 9.3 that the average player's liquid assets (regardless of the number of players) after playing 45 minutes (19 passes of Go) equals $1500—exactly what liquid assets were at the beginning of the game. If you keep a time-of-game clock and if you determine each player's liquid assets, you can figure out who has been lucky and who has not.

✱ **TACTICAL ADVANTAGE 19:** After 19 circuits, determine each player's liquid assets to identify who has been lucky and who has not. The dividing point between lucky and unlucky players is $1500 in liquid assets.

THE IMPORTANCE OF LIQUID ASSETS

Liquid assets are the maximum amount of cash a player could raise unassisted by liquidating all his or her assets (mortgaging all his or her property). To calculate your liquid assets, add to your cash balance the mortgage value of all of your unmortgaged properties.

When the game begins, all players have liquid assets of $1500, that is, $1500 cash and no property. Liquid assets temporarily decrease as players buy properties. Buying Boardwalk, for example, decreases liquid assets by $200, because cash balance decreases by the $400 you must pay the bank for the property, and the cash value of the buyer's properties increases only by $200, Boardwalk's mortgage value.

After most properties have been sold, players' liquid assets begin to increase.

CASH VERSUS LIQUID ASSETS

Cash on hand is a poor indicator of real wealth, and cash is a poor guide to help you determine your best strategic moves. To win, you must think in terms of liquid assets instead of cash.

✱ STRATEGIC ADVANTAGE 29: Use liquid assets—not cash on hand—to analyze your position in the game.

CASH FLOW AND TIME

Total assets, liquid assets, and cash all steadily rise at the same rate once the costs of the properties bought early in the game have been paid. To be wealthy enough to build houses and hotels on any particular monopoly, therefore, depends largely on whether you have played *long* enough before killer monopolies are formed.

Since most killer monopolies are formed by trades, you have some influence over when trades occur. You therefore have some control over how long you play and how wealthy you become before monopolies are manufactured. Of course, you do not have complete control.

When monopolies are formed before you would like them to form, you must have or must gain enough cash immediately, as opponents' monopolies will take all (or more than all) of the cash the bank throws your way. You face a cash crunch that, if you do not quickly solve, will cost you the game.

SOLVING THE CASH CRUNCH

Mortgaging ordinary properties is the most obvious and easiest way to raise cash, but the amount of cash gained may not be adequate, especially when developing one of the more expensive monopolies.

Another alternative for raising cash is to demand cash as part of the deal by which you manufacture your monopoly. Your trading partner will generally agree to this if the monopoly you give is more expensive than the monopoly you get. Unfortunately, your need for more cash is greatest when developing an expensive monopoly, and if you are forced to take the more expensive monopoly, you are most likely to be giving away cash rather than getting it.

✱ STRATEGIC ADVANTAGE 30: Demand cash from a trading partner who will gain a more expensive monopoly than the monopoly you gain from the deal.

∗ STRATEGIC ADVANTAGE 31: Offer extra properties to your trading partner instead of cash in a trade when you receive the more expensive monopoly.

The third most common method of raising cash is to sell individual properties whose changes in ownership would not create a monopoly. Your opponents will probably not fail to notice that any money you gain is likely to be used to buy more houses. Your opponents will therefore either not accept your offers or give far less than the face value of the property, in which case you would gain almost as much cash by simply mortgaging the property.

The trick to selling individual lots for cash is to do so *before* the monopoly chain reaction. You can in this way avoid the discounts that accompany property sales after the monopoly chain reaction. This requires a fairly accurate prediction of when your playing partners will be willing to trade, over which you have considerable influence through your own trading initiatives.

∗ TACTICAL ADVANTAGE 20: Try to predict when the monopoly chain reaction will occur, and time your selling of individual lots for cash accordingly.

SOLVING THE CASH CRUNCH
WITH RIGHT OF FIRST REFUSAL

Selling ordinary lots before the chain reaction could multiply the lot buyer's alternatives for trading for monopolies, improving bargaining power. Usually, it is in your interest not to make it easier for opponents to form monopolies. Your inclination might therefore be to avoid selling any developable lots, thus leaving only the Utilities and Railroads to sell.

You can minimize the undesired effects of such a sale by selling lots subject to the right of first refusal. The right of first refusal means that you, the seller, retain the right to buy back the property before the buyer can sell it to a third party.

When you use the right of first refusal as part of the sale, you in effect allow the buyer the opportunity to use that property to develop a monopoly, but you render the property useless as a potential monopoly property for all other players.

Such a sale also tends to draw the buyer to develop a monopoly out of the property you sold, which is acceptable if you believe he or she will not succeed in doing so or if you believe your monopoly will be more powerful.

＊**STRATEGIC ADVANTAGE 32:** Use the selling of lots subject to first refusal to draw an opposing player to developing a particular monopoly.

＊**STRATEGIC ADVANTAGE 33:** Use right-of-first-refusal sales to raise cash without multiplying chances for opponents to build monopolies.

SOLVING THE CASH CRUNCH BY SELLING OPTIONS

Selling options means that in exchange for giving you cash immediately, the player with whom you are dealing gains a right to one or more of your properties. The right could be to buy it or to obtain it free. There are infinite combinations of ways such deals can be structured.

You can propose an option deal whereby the option buyer may take a property at any time, or you can place limits on when the right may be exercised. You can propose conditional options whereby the right can be exercised only if a condition is satisfied. Here is an example of a conditional option: "If you give me $100 now, I will give you the right to buy Reading Railroad from me for $50 after you next land on it."

A variation of the "monopoly clock" can be used to make time-option deals easier to put together. Instead of using a real time clock, you can use the number of passes of Go or number of Chance cards drawn by any player to measure time. Here is an example of such a deal: "For $100 now, you have the right to buy Reading Railroad for $50 at any time after five Chance or Community Chest cards have been drawn."

Conditional options have the additional advantage of allowing you to use the expected-value formula (covered in Chapter 16) to mold deals in which you have superior knowledge about the real value of the properties.

* **TACTICAL ADVANTAGE 21:** Use sales of options to raise cash immediately before, during, or after the monopoly chain reaction.

To entice opponents to accept such deals, you must give opponents more cash and property than you gain. The advantage to you is that you gain cash when it is most valuable, that is, when you can invest it in high-profit houses.

RAISE CASH BY SELLING IMMUNITIES

An immunity is a right you give an opponent to not pay you some or all of the rent to which you are entitled.

Players are prone to think of immunities only after the building of hotels has raised the rents to dangerous levels. But immunities can be sold for lesser properties as well. If you own the Utility monopoly or three or four Railroads, rents are troublesome enough to attract buyers for immunities.

Of course, you will never have difficulty attracting interest in an immunity on developed property. You can make up for the rents not collected from the immune player by investing the cash the immune player gives you in houses, which increases your take from the other players.

Using the expected-value formula, you will often be able to price the immunity so that it is a source of profit to you of itself.

* **TACTICAL ADVANTAGE 22:** Sell immunities on weak monopolies and on killer monopolies to raise cash immediately before, during, or after the monopoly chain reaction.

PART THREE

MAKING THE BEST DECISIONS

Successful Monopoly play is both an art and a science. Monopoly is an art in that players interpret the words and actions of opponents to estimate what they have in mind. The game is also an art in that certain far-reaching decisions must be made by intuition or feel rather than by pure logic.

Some decisions that Monopoly players make involve choosing one of a limited number of options. When the benefits of every option are objectively known or can be known, Monopoly play can be scientific. How long to stay in jail is an example of such a decision.

In general, decisions that can be made scientifically should be made scientifically. An example from recent history shows why.

Only a century ago it was common for iron bridges to collapse under the load of a train or wagon. Railroadmen and teamsters knew this to be a hazard of their trades. Today, by contrast, no one feels endangered while driving over a bridge. The main reason for the change is that the art of designing bridges became an applied science, namely, structural engineering. Scientifically based decisions, while limited in scope, are less liable to be wrong.

The chapters in Part Three describe most of the Monopoly decisions that can be made scientifically. Players who know the factual pros and cons of all of their playing options can eliminate guessing what to do and thereby avoid making mistakes.

10 🚂

The Decision to Buy Property

Many players believe that the property-buying decision is simple: buy everything you land on. This rule of thumb is useful for new players, as most available properties should, in fact, be bought, especially in games with more than four players.

However, players who are determined to win more than their share of games must play by more complicated property buying guidelines. Buying property shrinks cash reserves that could otherwise be eventually invested in high-profit houses, so it makes sense to buy a property only when there is a good reason to do so. There are three reasons to buy properties:

1. To assemble a monopoly or to prevent an opponent from assembling a monopoly
2. To gain veto power over trades between opposing players
3. To gain a cash profit from your investment

Monopolies can be so powerful that gaining and blocking them is the first property-buying priority.

* STRATEGIC ADVANTAGE **34:** Always buy properties of color groups in which either no opponent or only one opponent already owns property.

All landings on unowned lots in the two-lot monopolies (Baltic and Boardwalk) are opportunities either to gain or to prevent a monopoly; therefore, it is in your interest always to buy when landing on these unowned squares.

> * **STRATEGIC ADVANTAGE 35:** Whenever possible, buy from the bank any lot in the Baltic and Boardwalk color groups.

ADVANCE YOUR CHANCES TO TRADE FOR THREE-PLACE MONOPOLIES

When there are more than two players, you will probably have to trade to gain a three-lot monopoly. It is much easier to complete a trade with one opposing player than it is to deal with two. Therefore, it is always in your interest to buy the second property in a color group unless you already own a killer monopoly.

> * **STRATEGIC ADVANTAGE 36:** Buy from the bank any property that will give you ownership of two properties in any monopoly group, unless you already own a killer monopoly.

WHEN TO BUY "VETO POWER"

In games involving three or more players it is possible to land on an unowned property in a color group whose two other properties are owned by two different opponents. Any chance for a natural monopoly had been destroyed before your opportunity to buy.

You should buy such a property if you do not own a killer monopoly *and* if you have no potential monopoly-forming trades with any one opponent *and* if the property would open for you the possibility of a "group grade." Group trades are discussed in Chapter 25.

The other situation in which such a property possibly should be bought is to prevent opposing players from trading later to form a monopoly involving that color group. Sometimes, buying the third property buys you veto power over one future trade. Such veto power is valuable if the property owners have no other alternatives for monopolies.

> * **STRATEGIC ADVANTAGE 37:** Buy the third remaining property of a color group owned by two different opponents when those

same opponents share complete ownership of one other killer monopoly.

When two opponents share complete ownership of more than one color group, obtaining veto power over yet another potential monopoly can be meaningless. It is virtually impossible to gain veto power over all potential monopolies. In this situation you must decide which of all the potential monopolies would be hardest for you to defeat. Buy the veto power property only if the color group containing the veto properties is the best of the monopolies that your opponents might manufacture. (Judging the "strength" of monopolies will be further considered later in this book.)

> ✳ STRATEGIC ADVANTAGE 38: When deciding whether or not to buy a veto power property in a color group otherwise owned by opponents, consider the strengths of the other monopolies in which the *same* opponents already share complete ownership. Buy the veto power property only if its color group is the strongest among your opponents' holdings.

You may remember from an earlier chapter that the New York monopoly is the most versatile. If you have no chance to gain that monopoly for yourself, it is worthwhile to ensure that opponents cannot gain it either.

> ✳ STRATEGIC ADVANTAGE 39: Extend your veto power over the New York monopoly by buying any property in the New York color group whenever you have the opportunity.

PROPERTIES AS INVESTMENTS

During the first 25 minutes of play, developable properties up for sale are usually good buys simply because they create, block, or veto a monopoly. Thereafter, however, you will have the opportunity to buy properties that do not offer any monopoly-building or monopoly-blocking advantage. Is it beneficial to take these later property-buying opportunities simply because of the rents the owner will enjoy?

A correct view of properties' value involves two ideas. First, the real value of rent income is not merely the cash opponents may have to pay in rent. An additional value is the cash the owner saves by not having to pay rent to an opponent. An owner who lands saves the difference between paying rent and not paying rent, which is two times the rent. Second, it is not necessary for rent earned and rent saved to add up to the cost of the property for it to be a good investment. It is only necessary for the amount of cash saved and earned through rents to equal the mortgage value of the property, as long as the cash profits come in before the cash is needed to pay for houses on monopolies.

When the sum of rents and rent savings equals the mortgage value, the cash balance of the property owner is as high as if he or she had not bought the property in the first place.

∗ TACTICAL ADVANTAGE 23: When deciding whether or not to buy a nonmonopolied property, estimate whether the totaled cash from rents and rent savings will equal the mortgage value of the property.

Since the monopoly chain reaction generally occurs after 60 to 90 minutes of play and since the decision to buy a property as a cash investment occurs after 20 minutes of play, a property must earn enough cash within 40 to 70 minutes of ownership, or else the property is not worth buying.

Figure 10.1 shows how much cash in rent saved and rent earned is generated compared to the mortgage value. For example, in 60 minutes of ownership (150 moves), Baltic generates $15 cash in rents and rents saved. But the mortgage value for Baltic is $30, so after one hour of play Baltic yields a cash deficit of $15.

You will notice that all developable properties except Boardwalk (which should be automatically bought for other reasons) generate cash deficits if the properties are owned for one hour or less. Only the Railroads and Utilities, the cash cows, return a cash surplus to the owner.

The significance of this is that only Railroads and Utilities should be bought with the idea of making a cash profit; all of the developable properties should be bought only to gain, destroy, or veto monopolies.

> ∗ TACTICAL ADVANTAGE **24:** Buy only Railroads and Utilities after the game is 30 minutes old, if the reason to buy the property is to generate a cash profit. Developable properties should be bought only to gain monopolies, to block opponents' monopolies, or to gain veto power.

There is an exception, however. If you expect to gain one of the less expensive (houses costing $50 or $100) monopolies, it is in your interest to buy additional developable properties. The reason is that you may not need to mortgage deeply to finance the cost of houses, so after the monopoly chain reaction your ordinary properties can continue to earn rent.

How do you know if you are likely to wind up with one of the lighter monopolies? First, if you own two of the lots in any of the cheaper monopolies, you are quite likely to end up with the third. Second, if you own fewer properties than your opponents, you should *try* to gain a lighter monopoly. (Reasons for this will be apparent later.)

When you know you will not have to mortgage to develop your monopoly, you can count on 90 minutes of additional play for nonmonopolized lots to earn you cash. (After 90 minutes fellow players are likely to go bankrupt, and you will again need all the cash you can get.)

The right column of Figure 10.1 shows how much of a cash surplus you could expect in 90 minutes. The figures show that besides the Railroads and Utilities, you can earn a cash surplus with all of the other properties except for the light blue (Connecticut) properties. But if you need to develop a less expensive monopoly, you should buy Connecticut properties simply to improve your chances for a low-cost monopoly.

> ∗ TACTICAL ADVANTAGE **25:** When planning to develop one of the cheaper monopolies, buy all of the properties you can.

FIGURE 10.1

CASH SURPLUSES OR DEFICITS FROM BUYING AND OWNING NONMONOPOLIED PROPERTIES

Nonmonopolied Property	Cash Surplus (+) or Cash Deficit (−) after One Hour of Ownership (150 moves)	Cash Surplus (+) or Cash Deficit (−) after 90 Minutes of Ownership (225 moves)
	($)	($)
Baltic	− 15	− 7
Reading RR	+ 169	+ 301
Vermont	− 24	− 10
St. Charles	− 20	+ 4
Electric Co.	+ 65	+ 133
Virginia	− 25	+ 1
Pennsylvania RR	+ 110	+ 281
St. James	− 20	+ 15
New York	− 14	+ 29
Indiana	− 19	+ 26
Illinois	− 9	+ 46
B&O RR	+ 172	+ 309
Ventnor	− 10	+ 50
Water Works	+ 63	+ 131
Pacific	− 29	+ 56
Short-Line RR	+ 110	+ 215
Park Place	− 20	+ 45
Boardwalk	+ 22	+ 133

Cash obtained by mortgaging properties plus rent earned from opponents plus cash saved by not paying rent to opponents' owned property adds up to the surpluses (+) or deficits (−) shown in this table. Nonmonopolied properties are those whose rents are never increased by houses and hotels. The table assumes that properties collect rent during entire period, i.e., that they are never mortgaged. Data are for four-player games. The surpluses are greater and the deficits smaller when there are fewer than four players.

SUMMARY OF PROPERTIES TO BUY

Here are the best property-buying tactics: Always buy the two-lot developable monopolies, the Railroads, and the Utilities. Buy the other properties only to gain a monopoly, to block a monopoly, or to gain veto power, except if you plan to develop one of the cheaper monopolies, when it is also profitable to buy all other properties.

Most players buy more properties than they should buy, especially after the first 30 minutes of play. You should not be surprised if my guidelines result in your buying fewer properties.

It may at first feel uncomfortable, but it is definitely in your interest to follow the guidelines and allow a greater number of properties to go to auction. The guidelines have been proved to result in more wins.

A set of 1000 experimental games showed that players owning monopolies are 33 percent more likely to bankrupt their opponents when they do not buy the third property of a broken color group.

Once the monopoly chain reaction is reached, what matters for winning is your choice of monopoly and your liquid assets. To the extent that ordinary properties decrease liquid assets, having more than your share of properties can be a disadvantage.

BIDDING AT AUCTIONS

The rules allow you to bid even if you were the player who turned down the chance to buy the property from the bank. You should always take auctions seriously because a property that is unattractive at its face value may become attractive at a lower price. Also, players occasionally bid stupidly, so all auctions are potential sources of bargains!

MINIMUM PRICE

Many players seem to stop thinking when an unattractive property is available for bidding. As a result, it is not rare to be able to buy a property at auction for less than $0 net cash, which means for less cash than the bank will give for an immediate mortgage. Since you can mortgage a property for 50 percent of its face value at any time, it makes no sense to let an opponent win an auction with a bid that is below the property's mortgage value.

✳ **TACTICAL ADVANTAGE 26:** Always bid a property up to at least

50 percent of its face value. Never let an opponent buy a property for less than its mortgage value.

BIDDING STRATEGY

Usually, properties that are available for bidding are relatively unattractive properties. Since players sometimes fail to realize that a property is always worth at least its mortgage value, start the bidding well below the mortgage value.

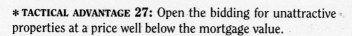

✳ **TACTICAL ADVANTAGE 27:** Open the bidding for unattractive properties at a price well below the mortgage value.

✳ **TACTICAL ADVANTAGE 28:** Increase bids for unattractive properties by small amounts, giving no hint to opponents that the property is worth at least its mortgage value.

Only after the bidding has increased to a price above the mortgage value is it necessary for you to think about the real value of the property.

The real value of any property that cannot be monopolized is the sum of the property's mortgage value plus the total rents the property can earn or save.

If you expect to mortgage the property immediately to pay rent or to buy houses, you should not bid more than mortgage value plus a few dollars. However, if you think that you will never have to mortgage the property, you should bid closer to the face value of the property (except for properties of the Connecticut color group, which are worth only slightly more than mortgage value).

Keep in mind the real, secret values of properties as detailed earlier. Generally, only the Utilities and Railroads are worth more than their face value.

Always consider the fact that the value of a property differs from one player to another. For example, if you can invest cash in additional houses, you should not bid much more than mortgage value in an auction. However, a player who has no other investment opportunities should be willing to bid more.

If the value of a property to you is less than the value of a property to another player, your goal in the auction should be to bid high enough so that the opponent with no investment alternatives does not get too great a bargain.

WHEN TO BUY UNATTRACTIVE PROPERTIES

Compare Premium over Face Value to Premium over Mortgage Value

Do not automatically allow an unattractive property to go to auction. Evaluate whether the property would give an opponent who has no monopolies a property that puts that player in a strong trading position with some other player. The property may be worth little more than its mortgage value to you, but it may be worth a great deal to one of your opponents—possibly much more than face value.

If such opponent is willing to pay you more of a premium above face value than you are willing to bid above mortgage value, you can propose a deal whereby you will sell that player the property right after you buy it. Therefore, before letting the property go to auction ask such players how much they would pay you for the property.

> ✳ **TACTICAL ADVANTAGE 29:** Before allowing a buying opportunity to go to auction, ask how much of a premium an opponent would be willing to pay you for the property. If the premium above face value is greater than the premium above mortgage value you are willing to pay, arrange a deal whereby you will buy the property and sell it to the other player at an agreed price.

Even if your opponent does not agree to pay you a premium for the property, you gain an advantage in that you will learn how much (as a minimum) your opponent is willing to bid for the property if you let it go to auction.

11 🚂

The Income Tax Decision

Every year in the United States more people are killed by pigs than by sharks. The Income Tax square is like the pigs—not feared but more dangerous than its reputation would indicate.

Income tax eats up about 14 percent of all salaries collected during a game. The Income Tax square is landed on about five times in a 90-minute game, so avoiding it entirely is not likely. It is easier to dodge income tax in real life than it is in Monopoly.

```
┌──────────┐
│ INCOME   │
│ TAX      │
│    ◆     │
│ PAY 10%  │
│   OR     │
│  $200    │
└──────────┘
```

There is nothing you can do to avoid the square, but you can minimize the damage when the dice force you to land. It only requires a little preparation to play the Income Tax square advantageously, and the work done for income tax is helpful in other, more important parts of the game.

There is only one decision to make when landing on Income Tax: to pay either $200 immediately or to pay 10 percent of all assets owned including property. The rules contain a wrinkle to make this decision more interesting. Once a player starts totaling net worth, he or she has committed to paying 10 percent—even if it means paying more than $200. That is why it pays to do some preparation before it is necessary to make the decision.

It is not necessary to count up your total wealth ahead of time. Simply knowing how income tax is calculated combined with knowing the basics of Monopoly cash flow makes it easy to decide whether to pay the flat $200.

The average player's cash flow during an average circuit of the board is $171. After three circuits of the board a player's total wealth increases from the initial $1500 stake to $1500 + ($171 x 3), or $2013. The $2013 total wealth after three circuits can be disguised by rents, property purchases, cards, and other cash transfers, but since Income Tax demands a tax on *all* assets, the tax burden builds up quickly and steadily.

After three circuits of the board, therefore, it is in your interest to elect to pay $200. Before the third circuit, it is better to pay 10 percent. On the third circuit of the board it makes little difference —you will pay about $200 either way.

* **TACTICAL ADVANTAGE 30:** When obligated to pay income tax, pay $200 if you have passed Go more than three times. Otherwise pay 10 percent.

This guideline holds true throughout the entire game, except for the period just before bankruptcy.

Late in the game mortgages can trick players into underestimating their wealth, and this can result in their paying more tax than is necessary. Mortgaging increases potential income tax. Not only do you continue to pay income tax on mortgaged properties just as if they were not mortgaged, but you must also pay tax on the cash you received from the bank for the mortgage.

When there are many players, it can be difficult to remember how many times you have passed Go. Income tax is another reason to use a game clock of dollar bills, as described in Chapter 5. Simply looking at your money pile will indicate instantly how many times you have passed Go. (Do not shuffle through your cash while on the Income Tax square as that could force you automatically to pay 10 percent.)

MONITOR THE INCOME TAX SQUARE

It is worthwhile to pay attention to what your opponents do when they land on Income Tax. First, many players have incorrect ideas about rules for computing income tax, and most of those ideas result in lower taxes. Second, many players make quick, quiet estimates of the tax owed, and those estimates are prone to be low. Whenever an opponent chooses to pay less than $200 income tax, insist on a full, accurate accounting. Not only will this increase your opponents' tax bills, but it will also give you a clear picture of your opponent's wealth.

> ✳ **TACTICAL ADVANTAGE 31:** When an opponent on Income Tax counts his or her assets "in silence," challenge the result and demand a careful accounting.

12

The Jail-Stay Decision

Jail is the best-known feature of Monopoly. Jail has proved to be so popular that inventors of more recent games have copied this feature. The jail in Monopoly is so well known that the expression "Go directly to jail; do not pass Go" has become part of our everyday speech in the sense of "Do exactly what you are told, even if you do not like it."

Most players think being commanded to jail is bad luck. But it is not necessarily so. When the board is teeming with opponents' hotels, jail is the safest, most profitable place to be.

Whether being sent to jail represents good luck or bad, when you get the command, you have only one decision to make: whether to stay in jail or to pay $50 to get out immediately.

Many players allow their personalities to govern this decision. Cautious, cost-conscious players are apt to stay in jail to try to save $50. Aggressive, risk-taking personalities generally pay $50 to get out of jail immediately. The correct decision hinges on the circumstances of the game rather than on personality.

PROS AND CONS OF STAYING IN JAIL

You need to balance the advantages of staying in jail against the disadvantages. There are two advantages to staying in jail:

1. You have a chance of saving $50 by staying in jail and waiting for doubles. The probability of doubles in any one of three dice rolls is 1 out of 2. So on average, you will save half of the $50 jail fee by staying in jail.
2. You pay less rent when sitting in jail, because you have no opportunities to land on opponents' properties. At the same time you suffer no reduction of rent collected from opponents, because the rules allow you to collect rents while in jail.

There are also two advantages to leaving jail immediately:

1. You will reach Go faster and thus collect more cash from the bank. The net cash gained from one circuit around the board is $171. Since it takes five turns on average to go around the board, a player who sits in jail takes a "penalty" of $35 per turn in lost cash flow.
2. If you throw doubles as you leave jail you may take the second turn, whereas you do not get a second move if you did not pay to get out of jail. (This is true according to the rules most people use.)

A player who decides to stay in jail will on average get out of jail after 2½ turns, while a player who pays $50 immediately gets out of jail at the first turn. This means that the player who stays in jail sacrifices 1½ turns, on average. Since one turn is worth $35 in net additional cash flow, 1½ turns is worth about $52. The decision boils down to this: Is it worth $52 in sacrificed cash flow to stay in jail to gain a chance to avoid the $50 fine and save 1½ turns of rent?

Further calculations result in this conclusion: it makes sense to stay in jail if the expected rent per circuit from all opponents' properties totals over $71. The expected rent per circuit for all nonmonopolied properties is about $80 if opponents own all properties. Opponents hardly ever own virtually all the properties, so it pays to leave jail early unless an opponent has a monopoly.

> **＊TACTICAL ADVANTAGE 32:** Pay to leave jail immediately if no opponent owns a monopoly.

THE JAIL-STAY DECISION IN THE FACE OF MONOPOLIES

The next relevant question is, how strong must opponents' monopolies be to justify staying in jail? You can determine the answer by calculating the expected rent for unmonopolied properties you do not own and adding to that the expected rent for all opponents' monopolies. If the expected value is above $71, stay in jail.

> **＊TACTICAL ADVANTAGE 33:** Stay in jail if the expected value of rents you will pay is more than $71 per circuit.

Fortunately for people who are not mathematically inclined, you need only follow a few simple guidelines to make a good jail-stay decision.

You should start to stay in jail whenever most of your opponents' properties are not mortgaged and any opponent has any monopoly stronger than two Railroads and two Utilities. This means that you should stay in jail if opponents own (1) two or more houses on any lot except in the Baltic monopoly, (2) four Railroads, (3) Baltic with hotels, (4) three Railroads, or (5) two Railroads and two Utilities.

> **＊TACTICAL ADVANTAGE 34:** Stay in jail as long as possible if any opponent owns a monopoly stronger than two Railroads and two Utilities.

THE GENERAL PATTERN

A general pattern emerges from following my guidelines. Early in the game, when there are likely to be no developed monopolies, you should pay $50 to leave jail immediately. Late in the game, when there are likely to be monopolies, the recommended general pattern would be to stay in jail.

Sometime in the middle of the game, you will want to switch

GO TO
JAIL

from *always* paying $50 to leave jail immediately to *always* staying in jail as long as possible. The jail-stay decision need not be made each time you land in jail. There is one unimportant exception: at the very end of the game, just before your last surviving opponent goes bankrupt, it will pay to switch back to leaving jail immediately.

> *TACTICAL ADVANTAGE 35:** Always pay $50 to leave jail early during the early stage of the game. Decide once when to switch your jail-stay policy to staying in jail. Do not switch the policy again until the very end of the game, when you are on the verge of winning.

EXCEPTIONS TO JAIL-STAY GUIDELINES

When you want to buy Electric Co., Virginia, St. James, or Tennessee, it may be better to stay in jail. The reason is that you have a better chance of throwing doubles, and doubles will more likely land you on the property you want. You have, for example, a 24.6 percent greater probability of landing on St. James or Tennessee if you stay in jail and wait for doubles.

The other exception occurs when you desperately need to land on a distant, unowned property. Staying in jail under such circumstances increases the probability that an opponent will land on that desired property. It may very well be worth the cash flow sacrifice to get out early, even if there are strong monopolies owned by opponents.

THE NEW YORK MONOPOLY: A SPECIAL SITUATION

If an opponent has hotels on the New York monopoly, you may hesitate to stay in jail because doing so increases the probability of throwing doubles 6 or 8, which puts you on the monopoly. However, paying to leave jail immediately entails another cost: you will circuit the board and reach the New York monopoly a second time quicker than had you originally stayed in jail. You can lose both ways!

The mathematical answer to this dilemma is quite complicated, so the details are not presented here. The answer is that you *should* stay in jail. Staying in jail is only about 4.5 percent less costly than leaving jail. However, if there are other opponents' monopolies besides the New York monopoly, the advantage to staying in jail becomes far greater than 4.5 percent.

13 🚂

Mortgaging Decisions

The mortgaging feature shows Monopoly's tie to the past. Monopoly mortgages were patterned after real-world mortgages of the early 1900s. In that era banks demanded 50 percent down payments. Furthermore, the borrower had to pay off the entire mortgage in three to five years.

Mortgaging is the only way to borrow money in Monopoly, so present-day Monopoly players must tolerate the financing methods of the past.

SENSIBLE BORROWING

Sensible borrowing means borrowing the right amount and borrowing at the lowest possible interest rate. Nearly all players innately sense that they should mortgage no more than necessary to meet a debt. Everyone realizes that it is senseless to pay interest on money that is not truly needed.

Yet players often disregard the "interest rate" on mortgages. They assume that all property mortgages cost the same. Although the 10 percent demortgaging fee is constant, the lost rental income varies from one property to another.

Compared to lost rental income, the 10 percent fee is a small part of your total borrowing costs. A single lost rental costs you about 18 percent of the property's mortgage value, on average. What's more, you usually need to pay the 10 percent fee no more than once for each property, whereas you could lose rental income any number of times.

THE SECRET VALUES OF PROPERTIES AND MORTGAGING

The real return on investment is relevant to mortgaging because the cost of borrowing (the interest rate) depends on how much rent is lost. The amount of rent lost is in turn proportional to the real ROI of the property, that is, its real, secret value.

When selecting properties to mortgage, you should mortgage properties with a low real ROI. Allow properties with a high ROI to continue earning rent.

✳ TACTICAL ADVANTAGE 36: Mortgage properties in order of their real return on investment (ROI). Mortgage properties with low real ROIs first and ones with high real ROIs last.

```
┌──────────────────[ FIGURE 13.1 ]──────────────────┐

                    MORTGAGING PRIORITIES

    Below-Average        Average              Above-Average
    Real Return on       Real Return on       Real Return on
    Investment           Investment           Investment
    ──────────────       ──────────────       ──────────────

    Mediterranean        St. James            New York
    Connecticut          Tennessee            Illinois
    Oriental             Indiana              Boardwalk
    Baltic               Kentucky             Short-Line RR
    Vermont              Atlantic             B&O RR
    States               Ventnor              Pennsylvania RR
    Virginia             Marvin Gardens       Reading RR
    St. Charles          Pacific              Water Works
                         North Carolina       Electric Co.
                         Pennsylvania
                         Park Place

    The properties in each column are listed in order of increasing real return on investment
    (ROI). Mortgage the properties in the left column first, those in the middle column next,
    and those in the right column last.
└───────────────────────────────────────────────────┘
```

Figure 6.4 in Chapter 6 displayed the real returns on investment of all Monopoly properties. The same data are shown in a different way in Figure 13.1, in which all the properties are divided into three categories: below average, average, and above average.

Properties with below-average returns on investment are basically overpriced and should be mortgaged first. By contrast, properties listed as yielding above-average returns on investment should be the last properties mortgaged. These mortgages result in a high borrowing cost, so avoid mortgaging these unless you have no acceptable alternative.

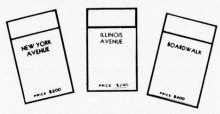

A PRACTICAL PROGRAM FOR LOWEST-COST BORROWING

Mortgaging properties in the order they appear in Figure 13.1, while theoretically ideal, is not very practical. No one is likely to remember the exact order of all the properties.

Fortunately, a general pattern emerges that makes it easy to approximate the ideal mortgaging order.

When you must borrow, mortgage properties in the order in which they appear on the board, but skip over the Utilities, the Railroads, New York Avenue, Illinois Avenue, and Boardwalk.

✳ **TACTICAL ADVANTAGE 37:** Mortgage properties from Mediterranean successively to Park Place in the order in which they appear on the board, passing by and not mortgaging the Utilities, the Railroads, New York, Illinois, and Boardwalk.

If you are so unfortunate as to need to mortgage yet additional properties, you will have to mortgage the above-average properties. Mortgage them in this order: first, New York, Illinois, and Boardwalk; second, the Railroads; and finally, the Utilities. If you own two Railroads, mortgage the Railroads last unless you also own the Utility monopoly, in which case mortgage the Utilities last. If you own three or four Railroads, mortgage the Railroads last. When you mortgage Railroads, start with the last Railroad (Short-Line) and work backward toward Reading.

> * **TACTICAL ADVANTAGE 38:** When forced to mortgage above-average properties, do so in this order: New York, Illinois, Boardwalk, Railroads, Utilities. If you own two or more Railroads, mortgage the Railroads last, unless you also own both Utilities, in which case the Utilities should be mortgaged last.

AVOID DOUBLE-PAYING THE 10 PERCENT MORTGAGE FEE

The 10 percent mortgage fee is payable only when you demortgage the property. Therefore, try to not demortgage a property you expect to mortgage again soon.

This advice most often comes into play in relation to properties you hope eventually to monopolize and develop.

> * **TACTICAL ADVANTAGE 39:** When following the suggested mortgaging priority, skip any properties you plan to monopolize or have monopolized. Do not mortgage such properties unless your only alternative is to mortgage Railroads or Utilities.

BORROWING MONEY BY LIQUIDATING HOUSES

There is, of course, another way to borrow money from the bank in Monopoly: you can sell houses back to the bank at half price. This is a painful way to borrow because the loan carries an "interest rate" of 50 percent, even if no one lands on your monopoly before you can repurchase the houses.

Almost no one sells houses unless there is no alternative. In fact, a house sale is often taken as a sign that the seller is close to bankruptcy.

It will surprise many players to learn there are situations in which it is wiser to sell a house than to mortgage a lot. This can occur when the only lots that can be mortgaged are Railroads in a four-Railroad monopoly and Utilities in a Utility monopoly and there are no more than two houses per lot.

The advantage of selling a house can be particularly great if you do not need all the cash that mortgaging a Utility or Railroad lot will bring you.

When you have a Railroad or Utility monopoly, do not mortgage them until you have studied the Title Deed cards for your developable monopolies.

* TACTICAL ADVANTAGE 40: When you are faced with mortgaging a Utility or Railroad monopoly property and you have developable properties with less than three houses per lot, consider liquidating the houses instead of mortgaging the properties.

DEMORTGAGING

Now that lowest-cost mortgaging has been fully described, it is easy to describe the most profitable way to demortgage: simply follow the mortgaging sequence in reverse.

First demortgage the Railroads and Utilities monopolies, followed by Boardwalk, Illinois, and New York. Finally, demortgage the remaining lots between the end of the board and Mediterranean.

* TACTICAL ADVANTAGE 41: Demortgage properties in the opposite order to that described for mortgaging.

WHEN NOT TO DEMORTGAGE

The order in which properties should be demortgaged is clear. Harder to determine is whether or not to demortgage properties in the first place.

Do not demortgage any property unless all of your monopolies are fully developed and you have enough cushion in the form of unmortgaged properties and cash to prevent any possibility in the near future of the need to sell houses to pay your debts.

* TACTICAL ADVANTAGE 42: Always fully develop your developable properties before demortgaging any nonmonopolized lots.

This holds true even if you own all the Railroads or both Utilities. The returns on investment on a fourth house or a hotel on a lot are always higher than the ROI of a Utility or Railroad monopoly.

Even after monopolies are fully developed, you should think twice before beginning any large-scale demortgaging campaign. Evaluate whether any of your opponents are likely to go bankrupt soon. If so, you will again need all the cash you can assemble in order to develop fully an additional monopoly that the bankruptcy might create for you. Mortgaging a property prematurely presents a potential waste of 10 percent.

> ✳ TACTICAL ADVANTAGE 43: Consider the possibility of forming new monopolies as a result of opponents' bankruptcies. Do not demortgage any but your higher-ROI properties if bankruptcies could gain for you another monopoly.

When deciding whether or not to demortgage, balance the costs against the benefits. In exchange for that 10 percent demortgaging fee, you gain the opportunity to collect rent, which averages about 9 percent of the face value of the property or 18 percent of the mortgage value—almost double the 10 percent fee.

Therefore, it is worthwhile to demortgage a property if you have a 50 percent chance of an opponent's landing on that property before you are again faced with the need to remortgage the same property.

> ✳ TACTICAL ADVANTAGE 44: Demortgage a property if you feel there is at least a 50-50 chance of an opponent's landing on it before you may need to mortgage it again.

Remember that the 10 percent fee you face goes to the bank, whereas the rent you may collect comes out of your opponent's pocket. That means that if you are not sure you have a 50-50 chance of an opponent's landing, you should err on the side of demortgaging.

To help you decide whether you have a 50-50 chance of an opponent's landing, you should keep in mind that it usually takes six or seven Go passes for a player to land on any one lot.

The fact that it takes six or seven circuits of the board for an opponent to land on a certain lot explains why you should *not* make mortgaging or demortgaging decisions based mainly on where on the board your opponents are located.

PSYCHOLOGY AND MORTGAGING

Mortgaging and demortgaging present the opportunity to read your opponents' minds. Nearly all players realize that they can save themselves 10 percent by not demortgaging a property, so all players tend to not mortgage properties for which they have important plans.

The same idea applies to the choice of property to demortgage. Demortgaging can be a clue that the property owner has plans for the property other than simply to collect rents.

> ✳ STRATEGIC ADVANTAGE 40: Take notice of the properties your opponents mortgage and demortgage. These could be clues as to trades they have in mind and what monopoly or additional monopoly they hope to gain.

If you choose to "hide" your wealth by any of the techniques described previously, you may wish to consider leaving one or more of your below-average properties mortgaged even if you can afford to demortgage and even if it would be in your interest from a cash flow standpoint to demortgage them. By leaving some properties mortgaged you can strengthen your image as a "poor" player.

> ✳ STRATEGIC ADVANTAGE 41: When you want to have the image of a struggling player or wish to add credibility to the small cash pile you display, do not demortgage all of your property. Leave one or two below-average properties mortgaged.

GIVE AWAY SOMETHING
WITHOUT GIVING AWAY ANYTHING

When approaching the monopoly chain reaction, it is helpful to be able to "give away" additional properties to close a trade. If you "throw in" mortgaged properties to sweeten trading deals, you can give an opponent a property that has little cash value at exactly the point in the game when cash is extremely important. Therefore, you can appear to sweeten a trade without actually giving anything of value.

> * STRATEGIC ADVANTAGE 42: Keep an inventory of nonstrategic properties in mortgage so you can trade away a property with no cash value.

14 🚂

Buying Houses

If Monopoly remains popular for a few more decades, the game is likely to get an award from the Linguistic Society for saving from extinction the word *house*. Marketers of various products have long realized that substituting the word *home* adds emotion and warmth to their sales pitches. Houses are now built by companies that call themselves "home builders." If you want to buy paint, you must find the "home care" department at the store. Today, even people who do not sell anything use the word *home* when they mean "house."

In keeping with Monopoly tradition—if not with modern language—this chapter is about buying houses, not homes.

THE ELUSIVE MAGIC FORMULA

All Monopoly players agree that you should always look to buy more houses. All players also agree that it is necessary to hold some cash in reserve. The trade-off between buying more houses and holding enough cash reserves is why house-buying decisions are among the most difficult that players must make.

Determining when to buy, how many to buy, and where to put houses would be greatly simplified if there were a simple rule, a magic formula, to follow. Finding such a magic formula was the first goal of analyzing over 60,000 games that were played specifically to test the various tactics for buying houses and are the basis of the findings reported in this chapter.

The major finding of these experimental games was that there is no magic formula in all cases concerning how much cash to keep in reserve after buying houses. In general, however, ideal cash reserves should be kept above $300 or $400 when developing the monopolies beyond Free Parking or when an opponent owns three or four Railroads. Following this policy, you can improve your win rate by about 9 percent. Ideal cash reserves can be smaller if you own a cheaper monopoly.

* TACTICAL ADVANTAGE 45: Do not buy houses on more expensive monopolies unless you are left with *at least* $300 cash in reserve after paying for the house.

* TACTICAL ADVANTAGE 46: Do not buy another house on any monopoly if an opponent owns three or four Railroads unless you are left with *at least* $300 cash in reserve after buying the house.

* TACTICAL ADVANTAGE 47: Resist the tendency to tolerate lower cash reserves when you have difficulty finding the money necessary to develop an expensive monopoly. Cash reserves should be kept higher—not lower—when you own an expensive monopoly.

DELAYING BUYING HOUSES: AN UNSUCCESSFUL TACTIC

Another question studied was whether it was beneficial to delay buying houses until there were enough liquid assets to put at least three houses on each monopolized lot. The rationale behind this tactic is that there is a big increase in rents when you go from two houses to three houses per lot. Furthermore, this tactic presents the possibility of surprising opponents.

According to the results of the experimental games, it is better, under all circumstances, to start to build houses immediately.

* TACTICAL ADVANTAGE 48: Do not delay buying houses.

THE FOLLOW-THE-LEADER TACTIC

Experimental games showed that to "follow the leader" was sometimes a winning tactic. "Following the leader" means not buying more houses unless you have a surplus of cash or if an opponent buys houses.

Following the leader is effective only when you own a heavier monopoly than your opponent. It is effective because a heavier monopoly gets more powerful in relation to its lighter competitors as time goes on and additional money enters the game. By resisting temporarily the opportunity to buy a house, the owner of the heavier monopoly may lull opponents into letting the game stretch unchanged a longer time before becoming aggressive.

> ✷ TACTICAL ADVANTAGE 49: Play "follow the leader" if you have the heavier monopoly and are short of liquid assets to buy houses.

THE ACCELERATION TACTIC

Acceleration in house buying means initially following a cautious schedule to buy houses until the first possibility of accumulating at least three houses per lot occurs, at which point all caution is disregarded. A player using an acceleration tactic will at some point mortgage all ordinary property and spend almost all cash on hand to place three houses on each lot.

Experimental games under many sets of conditions showed that acceleration was not a successful tactic. When acceleration was limited to situations in which an opponent was close to an ideal distance away for a monopoly landing, the results remained negative. Only when this tactic was limited to circumstances when the owner was only one house short of having three per property did this tactic stop being unsuccessful. Even then, its success was mild.

> ✷ TACTICAL ADVANTAGE 50: Do not use a "get three houses on a lot at any risk" house-buying policy unless you are just one house short of having three houses on every lot.

* TACTICAL ADVANTAGE 51: Be cautious about stretching your reserves thin when an opponent appears likely to land on your monopoly on the next move. No matter where a player is, he or she is more likely to pass by your monopoly than to land on it.

* TACTICAL ADVANTAGE 52: Consider where all opponents are on the board, rather than just the one closest to your monopoly. Consider accelerating your house buying when two or more opponents will reach your monopoly before you reach theirs.

THE MOST IMPORTANT HOUSE-BUYING QUESTION OF ALL

The house-buying tactic that has the most effect on winning is one that you may not associate as part of house buying. The key ingredient is mortgaging.

The effects of mortgaging were studied in about 24,800 games played under controlled conditions.

These games taught a valuable lesson. Usually, you will increase your chances of winning by mortgaging ordinary properties to finance the purchase of additional houses. The remarkable point is that the improvement in wins can be as high as 200 percent.

A second important point is this: do *not* mortgage properties if you have enough cash to buy three or four houses on each of your monopolized lots without mortgaging.

* TACTICAL ADVANTAGE 53: Do not hesitate to mortgage ordinary lots to finance the purchase of more houses.

* TACTICAL ADVANTAGE 54: Do not mortgage additional ordinary properties after you have already placed three or four houses on each monopolized property.

ENDING QUICKLY VERSUS STRETCHING

If players do not mortgage, games last longer—by 10 percent or more. Longer games favor the monopoly with the most expensive houses. Shorter games favor the monopoly with the cheapest houses.

Thus the ideal game from the point of view of the owner of a cheap monopoly is one in which only he or she mortgages and does so deeply enough to knock out opponents quickly.

The ideal situation from the point of view of the owner of an expensive monopoly is one in which only he or she mortgages and the opponents build houses more slowly, giving the expensive monopoly owner more time to build up his or her own monopoly.

From both points of view, it is desirable for an opponent *not* to mortgage heavily to finance the buying of houses. Therefore, one goal of all players should be to mortgage their own ordinary properties without inducing opponents to do the same. This is difficult to do, because all players feel uncomfortable if one player has many more houses than the others. Furthermore, if one player, who seems to know what he is doing, voluntarily mortgages, an example is established for others to follow.

THE MORTGAGING BLUFF

There is no way to hide your houses, but there is a way to hide or disguise your mortgaging so that your opponents do not follow your leadership and mortgage as deeply as you do.

If you buy a house whenever you get enough cash, you will be chronically short of cash to pay ordinary rent, taxes, and fines. This means that you will often have to mortgage to get relatively small amounts of cash.

To your opponents it appears that you need to mortgage often because you cannot easily pay ordinary rents and other small bills. In reality what you are doing is mortgaging more deeply to build houses without appearing to do so. (Another effect of this practice is to give you the appearance of a poorer player than you actually are. It thus serves as a wealth disguise.)

To put this bluff into practice, after you gain your own monopoly, do not mortgage quite as deeply as you otherwise could. Save more of your unmortgaged properties for individual, one-by-one mortgaging.

* **TACTICAL ADVANTAGE 55:** Use the mortgaging bluff to mortgage to buy more houses without appearing to do so.

It is in your interest to abandon the mortgaging bluff if an opponent goes all out to build houses with borrowed money. To keep even or exceed this opponent's expected rental income, you may have to mortgage property overtly to buy houses.

WHY MORTGAGING TO BUY HOUSES USUALLY WORKS

When you mortgage, you lose an asset that typically pays you 9 or 10 percent real return on your investment (real ROI). When you mortgage, half of your investment stays with the bank and earns no income for you. However, if you invest in houses, the other half can earn you much more income. Houses typically earn 30 percent to over 100 percent real ROI.

The reason players are afraid to mortgage properties is the downside risk. Whereas you can always mortgage lots and get them back later for a 10 percent fee, selling houses to the bank for cash involves a 50 percent "fee" that you can never recover.

The optimum balance between the benefits of mortgaging to raise cash for house buying and the risk involved with buying houses involves so many factors that no one will ever figure out a simple rule of thumb to guide Monopoly players. That is why Monopoly will never become simply a mathematical exercise.

RISK VERSUS GAIN

Many cautious Monopoly players have a simple way to decide whether to buy more houses. They look at their pile of cash and try to guess whether they would have enough cash after buying a house to meet their likely normal debts in the near future. If so, they buy a house; if not, they do not. For unusual debts, such as big rents on opponents' monopoly properties, they depend on being able to mortgage their ordinary properties.

Whether intentionally or not, players who follow this house-buying plan (which is not necessarily the best one) automatically conform to a logical way of dealing with risk: If you are doing well, take less risk; if things do not go well, take more risk. Taking risks in Monopoly is mostly the same as saying, "Buy more houses."

∗ TACTICAL ADVANTAGE 56: If the game is going well for you, buy fewer houses and let your cash cushion increase. If the game is not going well for you, take more risks and buy as many houses as you can.

BUYING HOUSES WHEN A MONOPOLY IS NEW

It is risky to mortgage properties to buy a group of houses when you first gain a monopoly. It seems safer to buy only a few houses initially. If you mortgage deeply and buy many houses, you face the possibility of going bankrupt quickly. An important question is whether the rent advantages of buying many houses fast outweighs the quick bankruptcy risk. To find an answer, look at Figure 14.1. It shows for two sets of experimental games the percentage of games won by Monopoly players who followed one of three different house-buying tactics. The player who mortgages deeply and buys as many houses as his or her postmortgage cash level allows does best. In fact, this player does *very* much better than either player using a different tactic.

∗ **TACTICAL ADVANTAGE 57:** When you get a new monopoly, the most successful tactic is to mortgage deeply and immediately buy as many houses as you can after allowing for normal expenses. Do not spread out your purchase of houses if you have a choice.

Player	Tactic	Situation 1 (% wins)	Situation 2 (% wins)
	FIGURE 14.1		
	COMPARISON OF THREE HOUSE-BUYING TACTICS		
A	Mortgaged and bought many houses immediately	30	72
B	Mortgaged and bought houses one or two at a time	19	58
C	Did not mortgage; bought one house initially	17	55

HOW DEEPLY TO MORTGAGE

You should mortgage deeply enough to buy immediately (if you can) hotels for the Baltic, Connecticut, and Virginia monopolies; for other monopolized lots, mortgage deeply enough to buy immediately (if you can) three houses per lot.

After reaching these levels, your first priority should become building a cash cushion. Do not mortgage additional properties. Buy more houses only after you have enough cash to pay any rent you may face.

> *** TACTICAL ADVANTAGE 58:** Unless you would have to mortgage Railroad or Utility monopolies, mortgage deeply enough to buy hotels if you own Baltic, Connecticut, or Virginia.

> *** TACTICAL ADVANTAGE 59:** Unless you would have to mortgage Railroad or Utility monopolies, mortgage deeply enough to buy three houses per lot if you own the New York monopoly or a monopoly beyond New York.

MAXIMUM NUMBER OF HOUSES TO BUY

It is not unusual to mortgage so deeply that your only unmortgaged properties are the ones beneath your houses.

Suppose that your opponent has developed a monopoly to the degree that if you land on it, you will not have enough cash to pay your debt except by selling some of your houses. In this situation you face the classic Monopoly dilemma. If you buy another house, you face the possibility of soon losing the house and another house too. (You can lose two houses for every additional house you buy because when you are forced to liquidate houses, you get back only half the money you paid.) If you do not buy another house, you face the possibility of not earning enough money to get out of your dangerous situation. The question is whether to be aggressive and buy another house or whether to conserve every dollar and buy no houses until you earn enough cash to pay rent without selling houses.

Understanding what is the best thing to do involves understanding two basic strategies and identifying which strategy applies to you. The first basic strategy is to "choke" an opponent so that he or she cannot earn the cash to develop a monopoly. The choking strategy is what the player with the lighter (less expensive) monopoly should follow.

The second basic strategy is survival. The survival strategy means that you do not care how much money your opponent earns; your main concern is to remain in the game as long as possible, hopefully becoming gradually richer. The survival strategy is appropriate for the player with the heavier (more expensive) monopoly. If you have the heavier monopoly, you will eventually drive your opponents to bankruptcy no matter how large a cash surplus they have, assuming that you survive long enough to develop your monopoly.

Getting back to the question at hand, if you own the heavier monopoly, you should buy the number of houses that maximizes your cash level. Mathematically, this means that you should buy the number of additional houses that maximizes the surplus of expected rents over expected house liquidation costs.

For the mathematically inclined, this means that you should calculate the average marginal rent increase from adding one house per lot and multiply by the number of opponents closer to your monopoly than you are to theirs. Divide by the cost of one additional house per lot. Buy additional houses as long as the ratio of adjusted marginal rents to marginal cost is over 50 percent.

This calculation tells you, first, never to buy houses if you are going to reach an opponent's monopoly before the opponent reaches yours.

✳ **TACTICAL ADVANTAGE 60:** When playing a survival strategy and facing the possible need to sell houses back to the bank, do not buy additional houses unless the number of opponents you expect soon to reach your monopoly exceeds the number of opponents' monopolies you will soon cross.

You must be patient to time your house purchase ideally. Wait for opponents to reach your monopoly's doorstep. Once enough players are near your monopoly, you must decide now many additional houses to buy. The calculation just given tells you to buy the third house on a lot, but only sometimes should you buy the second or fourth house. Do not buy the first house.

> ✳ **TACTICAL ADVANTAGE 61:** If you own the heavier monopoly, buy more houses if doing so gives you three houses per lot— even if by doing so you would not have enough liquid assets to pay an opponent if you land on that opponent's monopoly first.

Tactical Advantage 61 applies only when you face the possible need to sell some of your own houses and the timing, as described in Tactical Advantage 60, is ideal.

Facing Bankruptcy

If you are so unfortunate as to face bankruptcy the next time you land on an opponent's killer monopoly, you do not need to think hard about what to do. Simply buy all the houses you can. Not doing so serves no useful purpose except to make your opponent richer, when and if you go bankrupt to that opponent.

> ✳ **TACTICAL ADVANTAGE 62:** When facing bankruptcy on your next landing on an opponent's monopoly, forget about keeping a cash cushion and buy all the houses your cash balance permits.

Owning the Lighter Monopoly

When you face selling your own houses on your next monopoly landing and an opponent owns the heavier monopoly, you are in serious trouble. Owning a distressed, lighter monopoly means that you have already played the part of the game in which you are supposed to shine! If the probabilities of the game exert their expected influences, the worst for you is yet to come.

When faced with this situation, treat it as if you were facing bankruptcy on your next killer monopoly landing. Unless you can quickly force the heavier monopoly owner to liquidate some houses, you have little hope of winning. Do whatever is necessary to maintain hotels on your monopoly lots.

✻ **TACTICAL ADVANTAGE 63:** When you own a lighter monopoly and face the possibility of a rent bill you could not pay without liquidating houses, play as if you are facing bankruptcy. Follow the advice in Tactical Advantage 62.

WHERE TO PUT AN ODD HOUSE

The rules do not require you to have the same number of houses on each lot within a color group, though the difference in number of houses from one lot to the next must not be more than one. The question thus arises on which properties should extra houses be placed?

What to do with the first extra house is easy to figure out. Simple inspection of the Title Deed cards reveals that the last property of each monopoly group pays significantly higher rent than the other property or properties in the monopoly. It turns out that the increase in rent is greater than the landing frequency difference between properties within the same color group.

✻ **TACTICAL ADVANTAGE 64:** If you have an extra house, put it on the last, most expensive lot of the monopoly.

Almost every Monopoly player knows this. Not many know, however, where to place the second extra house on three-lot monopolies. The two choices always are properties that pay exactly the same rent. So it follows that you should put the second additional house on the property on which players land more often. This is the same as saying to put the second house on the property with the higher real ROI.

The real ROIs of all properties were displayed in Chapter 6, and the ROIs fell into an easy-to-remember pattern. Of two properties of equal cost and equal rent, the higher real ROI property is the property that is closer to Free Parking. (There is one minor exception to this: St. Charles Place. Because there is a Chance card commanding the holder to go to St. Charles Place, this property is landed on more often than its closer–to–Free Parking neighbor, States Avenue.) Therefore, always place your second additional house on property closest to Free Parking, but place it on St. Charles Place when you own the Virginia monopoly.

✳ TACTICAL ADVANTAGE 65: When you have a choice of placing an additional house on either lower-cost lot of a three-lot monopoly, place the house on the property closest to Free Parking. Do the opposite on the Virginia monopoly if the St. Charles Place Chance card has not been drawn or if you cannot remember whether the card has been drawn.

WHEN TO PLACE HOUSES IN FRONT OF OPPONENTS

Suppose an opponent is seven squares in front of Indiana Avenue and you feel you should buy two houses. Ordinarily, you would put the first additional house on Illinois because it pays more rent, and you would put the second house on Kentucky because it is closer to Free Parking than is Indiana.

However, in this situation there is one additional factor to consider. Your opponent is more likely to roll a 7 and thus more likely land on Indiana Avenue. Should you make an exception to the house placement rules and instead put an extra house on Indiana?

The answer involves comparing the probability differences between rolling a 7 and a number one higher or lower and comparing this to the percentage difference in expected rent for all your alternatives.

This calculation is too cumbersome to do in the middle of a Monopoly game. It is better to generalize. It turns out that you should generally make exceptions to the rule about always putting the extra second house on the property closest to Free Parking. You should not make exceptions to the rule about putting the first additional house on the most expensive property.

✳ TACTICAL ADVANTAGE 66: Consider where your opponents are when considering where to build houses. Make exceptions to the "build houses closer to Free Parking" rule if an opponent will land elsewhere by rolling a 7. Do not make exceptions about always putting the first house on the most expensive property.

15 🚂

Chance and Community Chest

Of all the Chance and Community Chest cards, only two kinds can be "managed" by a player: the two house assessment cards and the "go to" cards. You have simply to accept your fate when any of the others come up.

The reason cards are at all manageable is that if you know about the "card clock," the appearance of certain cards is predictable.

THE MONOPOLY CARD CLOCK

Monopoly has a built-in timer for you to use. It takes 225 moves or 38 circuits of the board to use all of the Chance and Community Chest cards once. That corresponds to about 90 minutes of play. But 90 minutes is an average that varies from one group of players to the next, and this is why keeping an eye on your wristwatch is not very helpful. But the 225 moves it takes for all the cards to show up varies only a little from game to game.

If you can remember the first card drawn in the game, when the card shows up again you know that 225 moves have been completed.

It is useful to have an alarm sound with the end of each 90-minute, 225-move segment because that tells you, if you recall, how much money has entered the game, and it can help you determine how much luck you have had compared to your opponents. An additional advantage is that this "card clock" can help you manage important Chance and Community Chest cards.

✳ **TACTICAL ADVANTAGE 67:** Use the cards as a game "clock" to help you set your bearings. When all of the 32 Chance and Community Chest cards have been used once, you know that about 225 moves have been completed. You also know that the cards will start to show up a second time.

Although most people can't remember the order in which most cards appear, most people can remember at least whether a noteworthy card showed up near the beginning of the game or just recently. If neither you nor any one else reshuffles the cards (and there is no rule requiring you to do so), you can gain an idea of when some cards particularly important to you will show up again.

✳ **TACTICAL ADVANTAGE 68:** Try to make mental notes about when in the game important cards first turn up so that you can predict when they will show up again during their second cycle. The important cards are the "go to" cards affecting your own developable monopolies and the house assessment cards.

This does not mean you can manage your game affairs so that you will never get stuck with a major expenditure for house assessments. You cannot develop your monopolies based solely on the risk of drawing a house assessment card. More urgent necessities usually exist. But paying attention to the order in which the cards surface can minimize your risk.

If you have a poor memory for detail, turn over the first card that you personally draw from the deck when you replace it on the bottom of the pile. If you do this adroitly, no one will notice, nor will anyone object to the gambit.

✳ **TACTICAL ADVANTAGE 69:** If you need to use a memory aid, return the first card you use to the bottom of the deck with its printed face up so that you will know and are reminded when 225 moves have been played.

WHEN TO SHUFFLE

The disadvantage of turning a card face up is that some players will, if they notice the card, shuffle the deck. This will prevent you from predicting when particular cards will turn up again.

Therefore, it is best, if you can, simply to remember the "anniversary" card. You thus provide no incentive to any opponent to shuffle the decks.

If you see a Community Chest or Chance card appear on the top of the pile face up, and if you were not the player who turned the card over, you should decide at that time whether or not to shuffle the cards. If none of the "go to" cards would soon send a player to a property you are developing and if a house assessment card would not kill your chances to win, shuffle the cards. This, at least, hurts other players' ability to predict the order in which cards appear.

* TACTICAL ADVANTAGE 70: In a game in which the cards have no tactical importance to you, shuffle the cards at every opportunity.

By this point in the game you will have hopefully established yourself as the game's rules "expert," enabling you to overcome any objections your opponents may voice.

ONE ADVANTAGE OF THE HOME TEAM

Frequent Monopoly players can become quite familiar with the order of the cards in their own set, and this is an advantage for the "home" player.

* TACTICAL ADVANTAGE 71: When playing on an opponent's board, shuffle the Community Chest and Chance cards before the game begins. When playing on your own set, do not.

16 🚂

How to Evaluate Offers

There are two types of deals or trades you are likely to encounter in Monopoly. Any offer you will ever receive or give in Monopoly is either straight or conditional.

Straight Trades

The most common offer is a straight trade whereby you give up one property in exchange for another property plus, possibly, some cash. Ideas for those trades are detailed later in the book.

Conditional Trades and Deals

The other common type of deal involves conditions, whereby what you give up or gain depends on what happens in some uncertain aspect of the game, usually dice rolls or property landings. An example is, "If you give me $500 now, I'll pay you double rent each time I land on one of your two Railroads."

It is very useful to be able to put a hard number on offers involving conditions. If you know how to place a realistic dollar value on such conditions, you can gain a significant advantage over players who can only guess or act on gut feelings. As you may suspect, to put a real number on something as uncertain as a conditional offer, you must know how to handle probabilities.

No Need for Alarm

Do not worry about treading into the world of statistics and probability theory. To gain a winning advantage in Monopoly, you need hardly any theoretical mathematical knowledge. You need only to add and multiply simple numbers, and generally you can do that in your head.

There is only one equation to learn to handle conditional offers, and it happens to be useful for many games other than Monopoly as well as for making decisions in everyday life. There are, therefore, benefits to you on a number of fronts for reading through what at first glance may appear to be a page of ugly mathematics.

THE ONE FORMULA ALL MONOPOLY PLAYERS SHOULD KNOW

The most important reason for Monopoly players to know something about probability is to be able to use the expected-value formula. Here are some examples of expected-value questions: How much rent will you collect from owning Water Works? How much money will you get from Chance and Community Chest cards? How much cash will you gain by circling the board? Should you accept an opponent's trade offer? How much is a certain immunity worth?

The formula, which is really quite simple, states that the expected value of a random phenomenon is calculated by multiplying each outcome by its probability and then summing up all possible outcomes.

EXPECTED VALUE $= a_1p_1 + a_2p_2 + a_3p_3 + \ldots a_np_n$

WHERE: a_1, a_2, a_3, etc. = possible outcomes of an event, expressed in numbers; in Monopoly these numbers are usually dollars

p_1, p_2, p_3, etc. = probabilities for each outcome: in Monopoly these probabilities usually refer to the likelihood of landing on a certain square or landing on a certain monopoly during one circle of the board

n = number of events

The formula can most easily be explained by an example. Suppose you are near the end of a three-player Monopoly game and each of your two partners owns a three-lot monopoly. Player A has three hotels on the Connecticut monopoly, and Player B has three hotels on the Illinois monopoly. How much rent will you pay on a typical circuit of the board?

Using rounded numbers, you will pay $600 when you land on the Connecticut monopoly and $1100 on an Illinois property. Assume that the probability of landing on any three-place monopoly during any circuit of the board is roughly ½.

EXPECTED RENTALS = EXPECTED VALUE = $a_1 p_1 + a_2 p_2 = (\$600 \times \frac{1}{2}) + (\$1100 \times \frac{1}{2}) = \$300 + \$550 = \$850$

This does not mean that you will pay $850 in rent during each circuit of the board; it means that if you circle the board many times, the rent you pay will average $850. This is the best estimate of how much rent you will pay, just as the best estimate of how often you will throw dice for a 7 is 1 time out of 6.

* **TACTICAL ADVANTAGE 72:** Use the expected-value formula to forecast how much money any player will (1) earn from his or her monopolies, and (2) pay opponents due to their monopolies. Find the difference to estimate a player's cash flow.

If you know how much you will pay and collect in monopoly rents and compare the difference to your cash flow from the bank ($171), you can predict whether you will become rich or whether you will go bankrupt!

Expected values give a great winning advantage when you use them to compare alternative actions. In other words, expected values are very useful in helping you make decisions.

MAKING DECISIONS USING THE EXPECTED-VALUE FORMULA

Suppose you can make one of two deals with one of your partners. You can have the Baltic monopoly while your partner gets the four-Railroad monopoly. Alternatively, if you want them, you can have the Railroads and your partner gets the Baltic monopoly. Which is the best trade for you?

Assume that you have enough money to buy hotels for Baltic properties, if that is the way you want to go. The probability of any player's landing on the Baltic monopoly on any circuit of the board is roughly ¼, while the probability of landing on one of the Railroads is ⅔. With hotels, Baltic pays $450, whereas Mediterranean pays $250 per landing for an average rent of $350.

The expected value for the rents from the Baltic monopoly from one player is calculated as follows:

EXPECTED VALUE $= a_1p_1 = \$350 \times ¼ = \$87.50$

The expected value of rents from four Railroads is calculated thus:

EXPECTED VALUE $= a_1p_1 = \$200 \times ⅔ = \$133.33$

The Railroads' expected value is far greater than Baltic's, even with hotels. In a four-player game, the owner of the Railroads monopoly can expect, on average, $133 in rental income at each circuit of the board from each of three opposing players. That is about 50 percent more than can be expected from the Baltic monopoly.

∗ **STRATEGIC ADVANTAGE 43:** When offered a trade or other offer, calculate the expected value for each of your alternatives. Choose the alternative with the highest expected value.

HOW TO FIGURE OUT THE PROBABILITY
OF ANY EVENT IN MONOPOLY

In the examples just described, you were given the probability of every event you needed to know.

There is no alternative to remembering a few representative probabilities. Fortunately, remembering probabilities for landing on any monopoly is easy. You may recall from Tactical Advantage 16 in Chapter 7 that the approximate probabilities are either quarters, fourths, or halves. (To refresh your memory, see Figure 7.2.)

It is also easy to remember the approximate landing probability for any single square on the board. During one circuit of the board the chance of landing on any particular square is 1 in 6—the same probability as getting a 7 from a dice roll.

> ✳ **TACTICAL ADVANTAGE 73:** Use 1 in 6 as the approximate probability of landing on a particular square during a circuit of the board.

WHY PROPOSE DEALS INVOLVING CONDITIONS AND PROBABILITIES?

You are likely sometimes to lack the cash or the properties necessary to induce an opponent to give you what you need to win. In such a situation your best chance to close a trade may be to figure out a deal involving some kind of future benefit or payoff that would be of interest to your opponent.

Here's an example of this kind of deal: "I'll pay you 10 times the rent if I land on States Avenue and my dice throw is an even number, if you give me Pennsylvania Avenue now."

> ✳ **TACTICAL ADVANTAGE 74:** Use probability deals as a substitute for cash or property to get opponents to trade you properties you need.

THE ADVANTAGE OF ENGINEERING COMPLICATED CONDITIONAL DEALS

It is to your advantage to propose complicated conditional deals to your opponents because social scientists have proved that people generally do poorly handling complicated issues involving risk. If the deal is complicated, you have a better chance that your opponent will overvalue what you are offering.

> ✳ **TACTICAL ADVANTAGE 75:** When you can, offer complicated conditional deals to opponents, as long as you know the real, expected value of your offer.

> ✳ **TACTICAL ADVANTAGE 76:** Refuse offers for deals or trades if they are complicated and you cannot figure out their real expected value.

FIGURE 16.1

PROBABILITIES VERSUS ODDS

Common language refers to the "odds" of an uncertain event, but here the term *probability* will be used instead. The two terms mean the same thing, but mathematically they are computed differently.

Odds of 1 to 2, written ½, means 1 success for every 2 failures. To convert these odds to a probability, add up the successes and failures to get the total number of events. Odds of 1 to 2 translated into a probability is 1 success out of 3 events, or ⅓ or 33 percent. Therefore, ½ odds equals a ⅓ probability.

The advantage of thinking in terms of probabilities instead of odds is that you can add or multiply one probability with another to get a meaningful number, whereas you cannot do so with odds.

Usually, it is more useful to know about the probability of two or more events rather than a single event. When dice rolls are involved, the calculations are simple.

"Either-Or" Events

To calculate the probability of an either-or event, add together the probabilities of all parts of the event.

For example, if the probability of landing on Boardwalk is ⅙ and the probability of landing on Park Place is ⅑, the probability of landing on *either* Boardwalk *or* Park Place is ⅑ + ⅙ = $^{10}/_{36}$ ≅ 25 percent (≅ means "approximately equal to").

"And" Events: Probabilities of More than One Success

"And" events are events that might happen together or right after each other. The probability of "and" events is simply the probabilities of the individual events multiplied by each other.

For example, if the probability of going to jail is ¼ and the probability of having to pay $50 to get out of jail is ½, the probability of going to jail *and* paying $50 is ¼ × ½ = ⅛ ≅ 12 percent.

Dice-Roll Probabilities

A discussion of probabilities in Monopoly would not be complete if it did not point out the probabilities of dice rolls. The chart below demonstrates that you need only to remember that the probability of a 7 is $^6/_{36}$ and the probabilities of other dice throws step down 1/36 for each number away from 7.

Probability	1/36	2/36	3/36	4/36	5/36	6/36	5/36	4/36	3/36	2/36	1/36
Dice Roll	2	3	4	5	6	7	8	9	10	11	12

HOW TO HANDLE COMPLICATED CONDITIONAL TRADES

No matter how complicated a deal or trade is, you can determine its expected value by using the expected-value formula. The only difficulty may be figuring out the probabilities to use in the formula. To calculate the probability of combinations of events requires an understanding of "and events," "either-or events," and "dice-roll probabilities." The way to calculate such probabilities is shown in Figure 16.1.

17 🚂

Managing Bankruptcy (of Others)

Bankruptcy, the stage of the game in which some players build houses while others go bankrupt, is often misplayed. After gaining a killer monopoly, many players concentrate solely on when and where to invest in houses. This is a mistake, because the economics of this stage of the game present another way to prosper and win.

THE ECONOMICS OF BANKRUPTCY

Soon after the monopoly chain reaction, the playing table is wiped clear of all large piles of cash. Weak players lose their cash to strong opponents, while strong players give their cash to the bank in exchange for more houses.

The demand for cash remains strong, because powerful players want to buy yet more houses, and weak players need ever greater sums of cash to survive.

The economics of this situation is determined by the law of supply and demand, which causes the value of cash to go up and the price of things bought with cash to go down. The prices of houses are fixed, but the resale price of all other Monopoly assets declines. Most notably, the cash value of ordinary lots goes down, so you can buy ordinary properties from your opponents for less cash than you possibly could in earlier stages of the game. Economists describe this kind of climate as deflationary.

The principal effect of deflation is that you can acquire ordinary properties for almost nothing, which means at a price only nominally above the properties' mortgage values.

Skilled players, who can occasionally divert their attention away from the exciting events of this stage of the game and focus instead on trading ordinary properties, are likely to find some bargains.

✱ **STRATEGIC ADVANTAGE 44:** Consider the bankruptcy stage as a time to acquire more property or to trade for new properties. Despite the shortage of cash players during this stage typically experience, additional properties can be affordable because of deflation.

WHAT PROPERTIES TO BUY

At this late time in the game, you cannot expect to eventually collect enough ordinary rent to make investing in ordinary properties very profitable—despite the bargain prices you can expect your opponents to agree to. You should try to acquire bargain-priced properties from your opponents for strategic reasons.

Some ordinary properties owned by opponents can lead to a new monopoly after bankruptcy causes properties' ownership to change. Other ordinary properties gain strategic value after a bankruptcy by suddenly gaining for their owner veto power over a new potential monopoly.

✱ **STRATEGIC ADVANTAGE 45:** During the bankruptcy stage aim to acquire properties that will through opponents' bankruptcies gain for you a monopoly or that will gain for you veto power over the formation of a new monopoly.

TAKE ACTION EARLY

It is hardly ever a surprise when a player goes bankrupt. The situation of those on the brink of bankruptcy is obvious to all.

If you try to acquire a property that will soon have strategic importance due to an impending bankruptcy, other skilled players will not fail to see what you are doing. They will bid up the price of the property, so that the property may no longer be a bargain.

THE KEY TO SUCCESS

To acquire properties at bargain prices you must make offers *before* it is obvious to all players that the property you want has strategic value. That is, you must propose deals before it is obvious that someone is going bankrupt.

> *****STRATEGIC ADVANTAGE 46:** When proposing deals for properties that will eventually be valuable, do so before it is obvious that any particular player will go bankrupt.

To propose deals early, you must be able to predict well ahead of time who will go bankrupt. This is the key to success in obtaining valuable properties for almost nothing.

PREDICTING BANKRUPTCIES

It has been proved by a huge set of experimental games that there is very little correlation between players' potential ability to win Monopoly and their rank among the losers if they lose. In other words, it is possible to predict who has the best chance of winning a particular game, but it is not possible to predict who will come in second, third, or fourth.

Therefore it is possible to predict who will eventually go bankrupt if no more trades take place. But you may need to be very patient to cash in on your prediction, as it is not possible to forecast the order in which losing players go bankrupt.

IDENTIFY SUPPORTING PLAYERS AND STARS

Let us refer to players with a good chance to win as "stars" and those without a good chance to win as "supporting players." Supporting players will, of course, eventually go bankrupt.

You can determine which of the two categories to place any opponent by means of the expected-value formula. Using the formula is easy, because once any player has built at least three houses per lot on a killer monopoly, ordinary cash flow and ordinary rents can be ignored. It is only necessary to estimate each player's expected monopoly rental payments and monopoly revenues. All players whose expected revenues exceed their expected costs are stars; the others are supporting players.

You must exercise some caution here when using the expected-value formula. Players with a sizable inventory of unmortgaged ordinary properties or with a large cash reserve could buy more houses at any time and thus could suddenly increase their expected revenues.

While you may have to revise your star and supporting player predictions as the game unfolds, you can expect, at least, to identify who is definitely a star and who is definitely a supporting player. In the first few minutes after the monopoly chain reaction the status of some players may remain uncertain.

WHAT KIND OF STAR ARE YOU?

What you should try to accomplish depends on what kind of star you are. Stars can be classified as upper-tier or lower-tier. Lower-tier stars own the Connecticut or Virginia monopolies; upper-tier stars own one of the heavier monopolies.

Upper-Tier Stars

As upper-tier owners develop their monopolies, they suffer chronic cash shortages. Therefore, despite the bargain prices, upper-tier monopoly owners should not spend any of their cash to acquire monopoly-forming properties. Only after obtaining more than three houses per lot and additional substantial cash reserves should an upper-tier star consider spending cash to get a second monopoly.

Up to that point, upper-tier stars should concentrate on blocking lower-tier stars from gaining monopolies, though sometimes it is possible to block or gain a future monopoly through one-for-one trades involving no sacrifice of cash.

*STRATEGIC ADVANTAGE 47: Upper-tier monopoly owners should follow these priorities during the bankruptcy stage of the game: (1) Develop your own monopoly and (2) block lower-tier stars from gaining an additional monopoly.

Not only do upper-tier stars lack the cash to buy properties that would gain a monopoly, they also have little need to do so. Most players who go bankrupt do so to an upper-tier monopoly, so upper-tier owners can reasonably hope to gain an additional monopoly without buying anything.

Lower-Tier Stars

The first priority for lower-tier stars must be to drain cash away from the upper-tier stars so that they cannot fully develop their monopolies. This means that lower-tier stars must build hotels quickly. Second, lower-tier stars should acquire properties that will form for themselves an additional monopoly after opponents go bankrupt. Third, they should block additional monopolies for upper-tier stars.

Lower-tier stars generally have extra cash to accomplish all this. They should not be afraid to give up some of their cash unless it would go to an upper-tier star.

*STRATEGIC ADVANTAGE 48: Lower-tier monopoly owners should follow these priorities during the bankruptcy stage of the game: (1) Build hotels, (2) acquire properties for an additional monopoly, (3) block upper-tier owners from gaining an additional monopoly.

THE SURVIVAL INSTINCT

If there are more than two players and you want to finish at the top instead of merely near the top, you must sometimes exert some control over how your weaker playing partners exit the game. You can influence when weak players leave the game, because most players feel compelled to survive, that is, to stay in the game as long as possible. They will accept almost any offer that allows them to continue to play, even if their chances of actually winning are nil.

The survival instinct in Monopoly is strong, because Monopoly treats losers rather badly. Players go bankrupt alone, so defeat cannot be shared with others. Worse yet, the losers cannot turn around and play another game. They must switch from being players to being onlookers. Only the second-to-last player, recognizing a hopeless situation, feels justified in resigning. All others hang on to the very end.

TO RESCUE OR NOT TO RESCUE

Each time a player faces bankruptcy, you must decide whether to invest in a rescue attempt. Because of the survival instinct, you can be confident the failing player will accept your rescue offer.

If a player facing bankruptcy to one of your star opponents needs only $50 or $100 to remain in the game, it is usually in your interest to come to the rescue with a last-minute deal that keeps the player in the game at least momentarily. The advantage to you is, of course, that the next time the rescued player lands on a killer monopoly, it might be yours, and you stand to take all that player's properties.

Whether to rescue a player from bankruptcy is a difficult decision when the rescue effort would cost you several hundred dollars.

WHO GOES BANKRUPT TO WHOM

It is important to realize that most players who go bankrupt do so to an upper-tier monopoly owner. First, of course, the higher rents on upper-tier monopolies make it more likely that a player who lands there will run out of cash. Second, lower-tier monopolies almost never throw a player so deeply into bankruptcy that a rescue is utterly impossible.

If you own a lower-tier monopoly, it is usually not wise to spend the money to rescue a supporting player from bankruptcy. Doing so makes it more probable that the same player, going bankrupt again, will do so to an upper-tier owner, who will ultimately end up with the cash you previously "gave" to rescue the weak player.

> *STRATEGIC ADVANTAGE 49:* Investing substantial amounts of money to save a player from bankruptcy to a star opponent is best limited to instances in which you have an upper-tier monopoly.

When a player faces bankruptcy to the strongest player, who will thereby gain a property that will result in winning the game for sure, you can point this fact out to your fellow surviving players. If a rescue effort would cost several hundred dollars, you can possibly succeed in leading a group effort to rescue the player facing bankruptcy.

✱ STRATEGIC ADVANTAGE 50: When a weak player facing bankruptcy is about to turn over ownership of a property that will certainly lead to a win for the player getting the property, consider leading a group rescue effort. A group of players who contribute to the effort can agree to share the bankrupt player's properties, if and when that player again goes bankrupt.

PART FOUR

DOGS INTO DIAMONDS, OR HOW TO TRADE YOUR OPPONENTS INTO OBLIVION

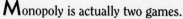

Monopoly is actually two games.

In monopolyless Monopoly, the tactical half of the game, players peck at each other repeatedly. Individually small tactical advantages come into play so often that within an hour or so of play, players making correct tactical decisions are likely to have become wealthier than others, though there is no guarantee.

Tactical Monopoly can be likened to a boxing match in which the more skilled player incessantly jabs at his opponent, while monopoly Monopoly is like a roundhouse cross to the jaw that leaves no doubt who delivered the punch and who took it.

If you leave monopolyless Monopoly as an underdog, you can still emerge victorious at the end with a knockout blow in the "second" Monopoly game.

The chapters in Part Four are about how to be on the happy side of a knockout punch. They cover four key issues:

1. When to leave the tactical game and enter monopoly Monopoly
2. How to evaluate which monopoly is best for you
3. How to get the monopoly you want
4. How to put it all together to drive every opponent into bankruptcy

18 🚂

Player Rank

Player rank refers to the relative wealth of the players in a game without monopolies.

Without monopolies, property-rich players get richer and property-poor players get richer too, the property-rich being those with the greater share of properties and the property-poor being those with a lesser share.

However, if property rents have more impact on player wealth than does luck, you would expect the property-rich to eventually grow wealthier than the property-poor.

RENT VERSUS LUCK

A total of 24,150 games were studied to determine whether rent or luck is more important to player wealth. The two players in these experimental games were perfectly equal except for a carefully measured difference in property ownership.

The results are shown in Figure 18.1. Even the slightest difference in property ownership, it turns out, is more significant than luck, when the game is played at least 78 minutes. (Virtually all Monopoly games last at least 78 minutes.) The conclusion from this experiment is that you can predict player rank by determining each player's relative rent income.

WHY PREDICT PLAYER RANK?

It is helpful—indeed, critical—to predict player rank because at a certain point in time, which depends on how much property you own, you must end monopolyless play and begin to assemble a killer monopoly.

Every investment made in an ordinary property involves a temporary decrease in the buyer's real wealth (liquid assets). A player who buys more than his or her proportionate share of properties remains less wealthy than property-poor opponents until sufficient time passes for the property-rich player to recoup half the cash originally spent to buy his or her properties.

Early in the game, property-rich players are both cash-poor and poor in terms of liquid assets. Once half the cash invested in properties has been earned back, the property-rich player is likely to have more cash and have greater liquid assets than the property-poor opponents.

Property-poor players must act to manufacture monopolies before property-rich players reach their break-even point. Otherwise, property-poor players will see their wealth and cash advantages turned into disadvantages.

∗ **STRATEGIC ADVANTAGE 51:** Always monitor whether you are property-rich or property-poor. Take notice of each of your opponents' status in this regard.

FIGURE 18.1

PERCENT OF GAMES LASTING 78 MINUTES (195 MOVES) IN WHICH PLAYER WITH MORE PROPERTY BECAME THE RICHER PLAYER

Difference in Standard Number of Properties Owned	Percent of Games in Which Player with Most Property Became Richest
+1	56
+2	59
+3	65
+4	66
+5	70
+2 Utilities	77
+3 Railroads	98

PERSISTENCE DOESN'T PAY

Every child growing up is taught the value of persistence ("If at first you don't succeed, . . ."). Such an attitude impels some property-poor Monopoly players to play longer, thinking that if they keep trying, they will catch up with property-rich opponents.

Unfortunately for property-poor players, Monopoly punishes persistence. The virtue Monopoly rewards is reflected by the saying "Make do with what you've got."

A CRUCIAL QUESTION: HOW LONG TO PLAY MONOPOLYLESS MONOPOLY

Once the break-even point is reached, the wealth advantage a property-rich player enjoys over one with few (or weak) properties grows larger as the game gets longer. Therefore, if you are property-rich, stretch the monopolyless (tactical) portion of the game as much as you can. The longer the game lasts before monopolies are manufactured, the greater becomes the wealth advantage you will enjoy over your opponents.

* **TACTICAL ADVANTAGE 77:** If you have more than your share of properties, resist the formation of monopolies. Make the tactical portion of the game last as long as possible; try to delay the monopoly chain reaction.

* **TACTICAL ADVANTAGE 78:** If you have less than your share of properties, cut the tactical portion of the game as short as you can. Manufacture monopolies. Encourage the monopoly chain reaction. Do not try to catch up by playing longer.

WHEN TO TRY TO CAUSE THE MONOPOLY CHAIN REACTION

It is helpful to have a feel for how long it takes players to collect enough rent to make a cash profit. This is the purpose of Figure 18.2. A cash profit means collecting more in rent than the amount of cash tied up in a property, the property's mortgage value.

As can be seen in Figure 18.2, it takes 225 moves or 90 minutes of play in most games for players to start to make a cash profit

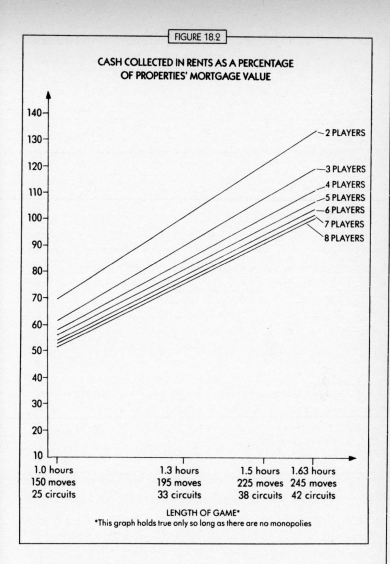

FIGURE 18.2

CASH COLLECTED IN RENTS AS A PERCENTAGE OF PROPERTIES' MORTGAGE VALUE

2 PLAYERS
3 PLAYERS
4 PLAYERS
5 PLAYERS
6 PLAYERS
7 PLAYERS
8 PLAYERS

1.0 hours	1.3 hours	1.5 hours	1.63 hours
150 moves	195 moves	225 moves	245 moves
25 circuits	33 circuits	38 circuits	42 circuits

LENGTH OF GAME*
*This graph holds true only so long as there are no monopolies

from property investments. You may recall that at this particular point in the game a number of "alarms" sound, namely:

· Players have a $1500 cash balance, on average.
· Chance or Community Chest cards begin to reappear.
· The game clock measures 38 circuits of the board.

* **TACTICAL ADVANTAGE 79:** Use the 225-move, 90-minute milestone to distinguish between games of a length advantageous for property-poor players from games advantageous for property-rich players.

* **TACTICAL ADVANTAGE 80:** If you are property-poor, try to trigger the monopoly chain reaction well before the game reaches the 225-move, 90-minute milestone.

* **TACTICAL ADVANTAGE 81:** If you are property-rich, try to delay the monopoly chain reaction until after the 225-move, 90-minute milestone.

MEASURE YOUR LUCK

The 90-minute, $1500-cash-balance milestone applies to both property-rich and property-poor players. You can use this milestone to measure how lucky you have been compared to an average player.

* **TACTICAL ADVANTAGE 82:** Take note of your cash balance at the 90-minute milestone. Having more or less than $1500 cash indicates whether you have had more or less than your share of luck.

MEASURE YOUR PROPERTY WEALTH

It should be clear by now that there is a definite connection between being property-rich (or property-poor) and (1) your rank among players in terms of ultimate wealth in monopolyless Monopoly and (2) the length of time you should play before trying to cause a monopoly chain reaction. If you understand these connections, you will appreciate the importance of always knowing whether you are property-poor or property-rich. Unfortunately, determining whether you are property-poor or property-rich is not as easy as simply counting properties. Remember that the real (or secret) values of properties vary greatly: you must take this into account when determining if you are property-rich.

Fortunately, there is an easy, accurate way of determining who is property-rich and who will rank as the wealthiest player.

The I2 Predictor

To use this wealth predictor, follow this procedure:

Ignoring Railroads and Utilities, simply count how many developable lots are owned by any particular player between St. James Place and Boardwalk. Multiply that number by 25 points, which is easy to do as everyone is used to dealing with quarters. Add to these points the amount of rent (expressed in points instead of dollars) the Railroads or Utilities owned anywhere on the board by that same player pay, taking into account that the rent (points) depends on the number of Utilities or Railroads owned. (Assume that rents are $28 for one Utility and $70 for each of both Utilities.)

This yields a number, the I2 number, that is proportional to any player's rent income. Compare the I2 numbers of any number of players and you can predict who will collect the greatest amount of ordinary rent or, equivalently, who among the players is most property-rich.

* STRATEGIC ADVANTAGE 52: Use the I2 technique to determine quickly which players can eventually become richer than others. Also use this technique to determine who is property-rich and who is property-poor.

As a point of caution, keep in mind what Neils Bohr, one of the giants of twentieth-century science, said about forecasting: "You can predict anything except the future." You cannot stake your life on the accuracy of the I2 predictor, as it is not 100 percent reliable. It is, however, accurate enough to stake a Monopoly game on.

For I2 differences of 50 points or more, the I2 predictor is accurate at least 75 percent of the time. For a 100-point difference, the predictor is over 90 percent accurate.

19 🚂

Tactical Trading

Tactical trading involves trading properties with little or no strategic value, this is, properties that do not help any player gain a killer monopoly. Thus tactical trading is limited to the Utilities, Railroads, Baltic and Mediterranean properties, and developable lots that have no strategic value.

HOW TO EVALUATE TACTICAL TRADES

There is only one thing to consider when you have the opportunity for a tactical trade: what it does to your liquid assets.

> * **TACTICAL ADVANTAGE 83:** Judge all tactical trades by one criterion: liquid assets. Accept a tactical trade if it improves or will improve your liquid assets; decline it if it does not or will not.

TRADES OF RENT

It is easy to see how a trade can increase your income from rents and thus increase your liquid assets. Rental income is cash income, so increased rental income eventually improves liquid assets.

An example of a rent trade is Connecticut and St. Charles in exchange for Ventnor. Connecticut pays $8 and St. Charles pays $10, for a total of $18 rent. Ventnor pays $22 rent. The player who gets Ventnor will enjoy a flow of rent $4 (22 percent) greater than that of the player who took the two less expensive properties. If not forced to leave the game soon or to mortgage, the Ventnor owner's improved rent income will eventually increase his or her liquid assets.

WHEN TO INITIATE TRADES OF RENT

Aim to complete trades of rents early in the game, when you can count on having enough time left in the game for rents to add up.

> ∗ TACTICAL ADVANTAGE 84: Trade for properties that improve your stream of rent income early in the game. Complete these trades while the bank still holds some unsold properties.

It is particularly important to do this type of trade early if the trade initially causes your liquid assets to drop, that is, if the face value of the lots you surrendered exceeded the face value of the properties you obtained.

HOW TO SUCCEED IN TRADES OF RENT

You will be a successful tactical trader if you keep in mind the secret values of properties, as described in Chapter 6, and if you focus your attention on the rent a property pays rather than on its face value.

Milk the Cash Cows

The biggest increase in rental income you can obtain from ordinary properties is to gain ownership of the cash cows, the Utilities and Railroads. It is not necessary to form a Utility or Railroad monopoly to make efforts to get cash cows worthwhile.

For example, each Utility, unmonopolized, pays $28 rent, on average—as much as any developable property on the lighter side of Pennsylvania Avenue. You can almost always gain a Utility for much less than the cost of Pennsylvania Avenue.

∗ **TACTICAL ADVANTAGE 85:** Trading for a Utility should be your first tactical trading priority to increase your rent income. Trade an ordinary developable lot for a Utility.

The second-best rent-income bargain is a single Railroad. At $25, a Railroad pays more rent than any property on the board costing under $300.

∗ **TACTICAL ADVANTAGE 86:** Your second tactical trading priority should be to trade an ordinary developable lot for a Railroad.

You are not likely to have opponents so foolish as to give you in exchange for a developable lot a second Railroad or Utility, that is, a minor monopoly. You probably would have to give in exchange a second or third ordinary lot, which would nevertheless be a worthwhile trade for you.

Try to Form a Minor Monopoly—a Cash-Cow Monopoly

Three Railroads pull in as much rent as 15 ordinary developable lots! Four Railroads pull in more rent than all the ordinary developable lots on the board combined! Obviously, you almost never own enough ordinary properties to give to an opponent enough ordinary lots to compensate fairly for giving you a third or fourth Railroad.

However, your main purpose is not to treat opponents fairly; your main purpose is to make opponents go bankrupt. Therefore, your third tactical trading priority should be to form a Utility or Railroad monopoly by trading away many or all of your ordinary developable lots that would not give your opponent a killer monopoly.

∗ **TACTICAL ADVANTAGE 87:** Be "generous" and offer to give away all of your properties that would not create killer monopolies in exchange for a third or fourth Railroad.

✳ TACTICAL ADVANTAGE 88: Give away up to five ordinary, non-strategic developable lots in exchange for a second Utility.

It is very possible (indeed, it is likely, if all opponents are skilled players) that no opponent will give you a cash-cow monopoly in exchange for any number of ordinary, developable lots. In that case, you should try to form a minor monopoly by trading one of your cash cows for an opponent's cash cow. Such a deal is easy to accomplish if you own at least one Utility and one Railroad.

✳ TACTICAL ADVANTAGE 89: If you and your opponent each owns only one Railroad, trade away your Railroad for the second Utility.

🚂 🚂 🚂

✳ TACTICAL ADVANTAGE 90: Trade away a Utility to the player who owns the other Utility to gain a third or fourth Railroad.

You can use the expected-value formula to devise other advantageous deals involving a combination of developable ordinary lots and cash cows.

Reduce the Number of Ordinary Lots You Own

Once you have done what you can to gain cash cows and minor monopolies, you should look to trades involving ordinary developable lots.

How to gain a rent advantage by trading ordinary developable lots can be stated this way: Offer to trade two or more cheaper lots to get one more expensive lot whose face value is approximately equal to the sum of the face values of the cheaper lots. Alternately, aim to take a more expensive lot in exchange for a cheaper lot plus a sum of cash that equalizes the face values of the properties traded. In both cases, you should take the more expensive properties.

✳ TACTICAL ADVANTAGE 91: To gain a rent advantage, trade cheaper properties for a smaller number of more expensive properties whose face value roughly equals the sum of the face values of the cheaper properties.

Another way of looking at Tactical Advantage 91 is to trade for one bigger rent from a number of smaller rents that add up to no more than the big rent.

What should you do if the little rents equal or slightly exceed the bigger rent? Consider the landing frequency. Take the property closer to Free Parking.

⁕ TACTICAL ADVANTAGE 92: In case of a tie or near-tie between the sum of rents of cheaper properties and the more expensive property, take the property (or properties) closest to Free Parking.

Use a Little Convincing Nonsense

Sometimes it pays to be irrational. If a trading partner points out that the rent of the more expensive property is more than the combined rents of the cheaper properties, mention that the cheaper properties, because there are more of them, will be collectively landed on more often. This point is nonsense, but it can be convincing nonsense.

TRADING PROPERTIES WHEN APPROACHING THE MONOPOLY CHAIN REACTION

Once players come close to the time they will build houses, rents become unimportant.

At this point, if you are poor, you should disregard rents and trade on the basis of mortgage value. Take in trade any group of properties whose total mortgage value exceeds (or any amount of cash that exceeds) the mortgage value of the properties you give away.

For example, sell Pacific Avenue (face value $300, mortgage value $150) for $200. You thus gain $50 in cash over mortgage value.

At first this may appear to be an example of a poor trade for the player who first owned Pacific. However, you must consider what will happen to the extra $50 cash the Pacific owner gained. If the

$50 helps buy an additional house, it is possible that the $50 may within a few minutes increase rents collected by $50, $100, or more.

> ✳ **TACTICAL ADVANTAGE 93:** When you have a monopoly but no hotels (or if you will soon have a monopoly without hotels), trade ordinary properties for any reasonable amount of cash greater than the properties' mortgage value.

20

Mysterious Monopoly Traits Exposed

Success in winning Monopoly is not unlike the adage about success in business. Success requires being at the right place at the right time. To win Monopoly you must buy a monopoly at the right place on the board at the right time. If either your timing or your choice of monopoly is wrong, you are liable to go bankrupt.

Unless Monopoly is still new to you, you undoubtedly realize it is better to buy the inexpensive monopolies when you have little money and to buy expensive monopolies when you are rich. This is the same as saying you should follow this rule of thumb: settle for cheap monopolies early in the game and take an expensive monopoly only late in the game.

Several generations of Monopoly players have followed this rule of thumb. Yet everyone who plays Monopoly frequently has noticed that similar games can have very dissimilar outcomes. This suggests that it takes more than one simple rule of thumb to win Monopoly consistently.

A typical player has a clear memory of only a handful of recent games. Unless you can see the results of thousands of games, the wins and losses produced by monopolies can indeed appear mysterious.

THE ULTIMATE MONOPOLY TOURNAMENT

To unlock the mysterious ways monopolies win and lose, two sets of experimental games were played using computer simulation.

The One-on-One Monopoly Tournament

The first set of experimental games involved two players who in each of over 200 different game situations played each other often enough (over 40,000 times) to neutralize all effects of luck.

Just as one-on-one basketball pits one player against another without teammates to help or hinder either player, one-on-one Monopoly involved one isolated monopoly versus another isolated monopoly. All other factors such as starting order, cash, and ordinary rent advantages were neutralized.

Rather than burden you with pages full of numbers, the results are presented here graphically. The graphs allow you to read what percentage of games were won by any monopoly at various levels of player wealth. The measure of player wealth in the graph is liquid assets.

The Checkmark Curve

Figure 20.1 is a graph of a typical one-on-one game. This graph shows what happens when the Virginia and Pennsylvania monopolies, formed simultaneously, compete against each other. The curve looks like a checkmark with a short nose. The curve is typical for any battle between two monopolies when the vertical axis measures the win percentage of the more expensive monopoly.

The curve shows that when liquid assets are close to zero when the monopolies are formed, Pennsylvania wins only a small percentage of games.

By contrast, when owners at the time the monopolies are formed have at least $2878 in liquid assets, the Pennsylvania owner has the better chance of winning. At $2878 in liquid assets each, they evenly split the wins.

The far-left nose of the checkmark curve always occurs at liquid-asset levels below $1000. It is rare to get a monopoly when your liquid assets are that low, so not all the checkmark curves shown in this chapter show the nose of the checkmark.

Except at the nose of the checkmark, the owner of the heavier monopoly, by being richer, always improves the probability of winning.

The 50-50 Point

At a certain level of liquid assets, the owners of a pair of monopo-

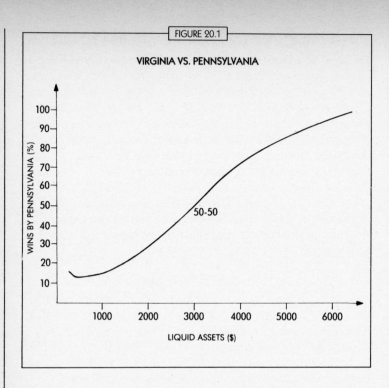

FIGURE 20.1

VIRGINIA VS. PENNSYLVANIA

y-axis: WINS BY PENNSYLVANIA (%)

x-axis: LIQUID ASSETS ($)

50-50

lies split the wins evenly. Let's call this amount of liquid assets the 50-50 point.

> *** STRATEGIC ADVANTAGE 53:** Before (to the left of) the 50-50 point, you should try to gain the cheaper monopoly. Above (to the right of) the 50-50 point, you should take the more expensive monopoly.

Having seen what a light monopoly such as Virginia can do against a heavy monopoly like Pennsylvania (which is actually the heaviest of the heavy monopolies), it is easy to see the folly of always trying to gain the most expensive monopoly. To win Monopoly, try to gain ownership of a monopoly while your liquid assets are on the favorable side of the 50-50 point.

Take Advantage of Your Opponent's Dreams of Huge Rents

Players have a sharp mental image of the huge rents they can earn by owning one of the heavier monopolies. The idea that an expensive monopoly is worthless if not developed is not nearly as vivid. If you keep the checkmark curve in mind, you can take advantage of the preference most players naturally feel toward the heavier monopolies. Tempt your opponents to take a heavy monopoly, and it is likely that they will at least partially disregard the fact that they do not have the liquid assets necessary to exploit the heavy monopoly.

> ✳ **STRATEGIC ADVANTAGE 54:** Induce opponents to take a heavy monopoly at a point in the game when only your monopoly (a lighter monopoly) can be fully exploited.

Even after having realized that a monopoly is too expensive, an opponent may nevertheless accept a trade whereby you gain a monopoly that can be better developed initially. Your opponent is probably hoping to develop the expensive monopoly gradually—though that hope is probably without foundation. It has been mentioned previously but deserves repeating: once any one killer monopoly has been at least 50 percent developed (three or more houses on any property), all players can expect to live and die by the strength of their own monopolies. Without three or more houses, any player facing opponents with three or more houses on a lot can expect to become poorer and to be unable to further develop his or her own monopoly.

> ✳ **STRATEGIC ADVANTAGE 55:** Take advantage of opponents' hopes and intentions to build their new killer monopolies gradually. Offer them the chance to do so; many hope that their cash flow from passing Go, Chance and Community Chest cards, and the like will enable them to buy additional houses.

THE ROUND-ROBIN ONE-ON-ONE MONOPOLY TOURNAMENT

Timing and Light Monopolies

Figure 20.2 shows what happens when the two lightest killer monopolies, Connecticut and Virginia, square off against each other. The checkmark curve is steep. This means that you must be careful about the liquid assets in the game. A relatively small change in liquid assets makes a big difference in how the owners of these two monopolies divide the wins between themselves.

A steep checkmark curve is characteristic of all games involving one of the cheaper monopolies.

> ✳ **STRATEGIC ADVANTAGE 56:** Pay particular attention to *when* monopolies are created, if one of the new monopolies is Virginia or Connecticut, as these monopolies have steep checkmark curves.

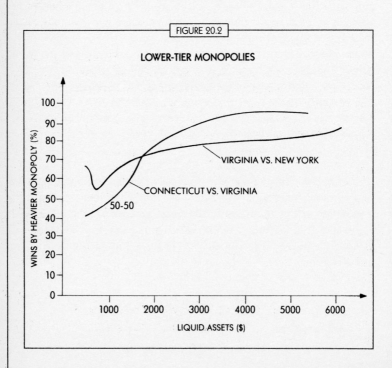

FIGURE 20.2

LOWER-TIER MONOPOLIES

The Weak Sister

Figure 20.2 also shows what happens when Virginia and New York monopolies do battle. The checkmark curve is not steep, so the point in time that these two monopolies are formed is not particularly important.

Note that there is no 50-50 point. New York always wins most of the games, whatever the players' liquid assets. Many players look at Virginia and New York monopolies as twins, though most players prefer New York because of its higher rents. Actually, Virginia is a weak sister rather than a twin sister of New York. New York's properties are landed on more often than Virginia's, and this, combined with New York's larger rents, enables New York always to dominate Virginia.

THE UPPER TIER

Figure 20.3 completes this one-on-one monopoly tournament. All of these monopolies are in the same league; New York, Boardwalk, Illinois, Marvin Gardens, and Pennsylvania form the upper tier of Monopoly monopolies.

The curves of games involving all monopolies from New York to Boardwalk are similar and are not steeply sloped. This means that you cannot with a high degree of confidence defeat an upper-tier monopoly with another upper-tier monopoly unless you have very low or very high liquid assets or unless you have an advantage elsewhere on the board.

Another Weak Sister

Many players believe that Marvin Gardens is a better monopoly than Illinois because of Marvin Gardens' higher rents. Illinois' properties are landed on more frequently, however, and this fact cancels out Marvin Gardens' higher rents. After plenty of money has entered the game, Illinois and Marvin Gardens are virtually equal, with a slight edge for Illinois. Early in the game, Illinois is definitely the stronger monopoly.

Don't Be Fooled by Boardwalk

Figure 20.3 shows that Boardwalk plays like a light monopoly against Pennsylvania but like a heavy monopoly against New York.

So despite its position at the end of the board, Boardwalk is not actually the heaviest or most costly monopoly.

Boardwalk was placed where it is on the board for symmetry, that is, to make the board prettier. It would be a mistake, however, to play the game as if Boardwalk were the costliest monopoly. The $2000 rent of Boardwalk fools many players into believing that Boardwalk is a very expensive monopoly. It actually "plays" cheaper than Pennsylvania, Marvin Gardens, and Illinois.

    * **STRATEGIC ADVANTAGE 57:** Treat Boardwalk as if it were a monopoly slightly more costly than New York and less costly than Illinois.

If Boardwalk was placed on the board in relation to how it plays against other monopolies, Park Place would be directly on top of New York Avenue and Boardwalk would be on top of Free Parking.

Figure 20.3 shows that Boardwalk never wins as many as 50 percent of its games against New York. However, Boardwalk is a twin sister of New York rather than a weak sister. Boardwalk in its own right is a versatile, powerful monopoly.

Where you should visualize Boardwalk on the board is not a trivial matter. Once you think of Boardwalk as located at the Free Parking square, each successive monopoly on the board becomes heavier than its predecessor and has a higher 50-50 point. The board itself becomes a reminder to analyze the relative strengths of monopolies properly.

IDENTIFYING 50-50 POINTS

For 50-50 points to be useful, you must know quite exactly the 50-50 point between any pair of developable monopolies. There are 28 pairs of developable monopolies you may have to worry about.

Fortunately, you do not have to remember 28 monopoly pairs and of each their 50-50 points. Simply remember this: when you could (after mortgaging all of your nonmonopolized properties) buy hotels at $1000 apiece for each lot of an upper-tier monopoly, you are on the side of the 50-50 point where the advantage belongs to the heavier monopoly. (Hotels cost $1000 apiece for the Pennsylvania and Boardwalk monopolies, but this rule of thumb applies

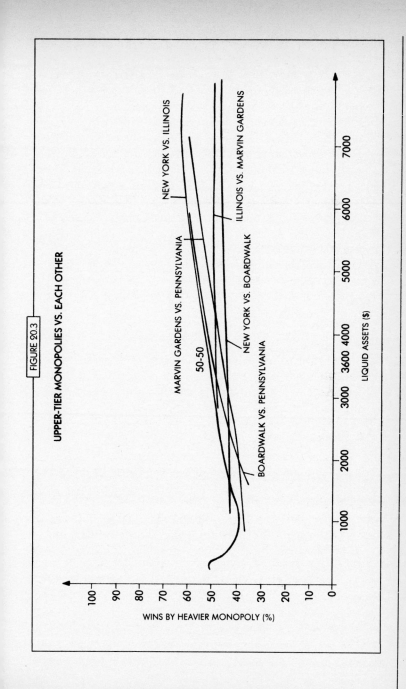

FIGURE 20.3

UPPER-TIER MONOPOLIES VS. EACH OTHER

NEW YORK VS. ILLINOIS

ILLINOIS VS. MARVIN GARDENS

MARVIN GARDENS VS. PENNSYLVANIA

50-50

NEW YORK VS. BOARDWALK

BOARDWALK VS. PENNSYLVANIA

WINS BY HEAVIER MONOPOLY (%)

LIQUID ASSETS ($)

to all upper-tier monopolies, not just Pennsylvania and Board-walk.)

When using this rule to compare two upper-tier monopolies, evaluate the heavier monopoly against the liquid assets of the player who is to gain the heavier monopoly.

To figure out if you have liquid assets sufficient to buy "Pennsylvania-priced" hotels for the monopoly in which you are interested, follow these steps: (1) Calculate how much cash you (or the potential owner) could raise by mortgaging all properties except for the lots of the monopoly itself. (2) Add to this the amount of cash on hand. (3) Compare this to the amount that would be needed to buy (at $200 each) four houses and a hotel on each lot.

> ∗ STRATEGIC ADVANTAGE 58: To determine the 50-50 point of any pair of upper-tier monopolies, calculate whether its owner could buy hotels costing $1000 each on each lot of the monopoly. If so, the owner has passed the 50-50 point.

THE HOTEL RULE

It is convenient to call Strategic Advantage 58 the "hotel rule." Note that this rule does not say that you or your opponent must immediately buy hotels; it simply says that you should evaluate whether such a purchase would be possible.

The hotel rule applies to all monopolies except the two cheapest killer monopolies, Connecticut and Virginia.

> ∗ STRATEGIC ADVANTAGE 59: Use the hotel rule to evaluate trades by which you and an opponent each gain one monopoly. Take the heavier monopoly if you are above the 50-50 point, the lighter one if you are below the 50-50 point. If both of a pair of monopolies are above the 50-50 point, take the heavier monopoly; if both are below the 50-50 point, take the lighter monopoly.

THE THREE-HOUSE RULE

If you have a choice between a pair of monopolies one of which is Virginia or Connecticut, the hotel rule does not apply. Instead, you must use another rule to determine the 50-50 point. Instead of the ability to buy hotels, consider whether you would have enough liquid assets to buy three houses on each of the lots of the heavier monopoly.

 ✱ STRATEGIC ADVANTAGE 60: When determining the 50-50 point between two monopolies and one of the monopolies is Connecticut or Virginia, use the following criteria: If you can afford to buy three houses on the heavier monopoly after having liquidated all your ordinary properties, you have passed the 50-50 point. If not, you are still short of the 50-50 point.

When calculating how many houses you could buy for purposes of the three-house rule, use the actual cost of the monopoly in question. For example, when you are interested in knowing the 50-50 point between Illinois and Virginia, use $150 per house.

For convenience, let us refer to Strategic Advantage 60 as the "three-house rule." When evaluating whether or not to take the Virginia or Connecticut monopoly in a trade that creates two monopolies, use the three-house rule just as you would use the hotel rule in connection with trades involving two upper-tier monopolies.

 ✱ STRATEGIC ADVANTAGE 61: When evaluating trades that create two monopolies, one being either Connecticut or Virginia, take the heavier monopoly if you are above the 50-50 point; otherwise take the lighter monopoly.

 ✱ STRATEGIC ADVANTAGE 62: When evaluating trades that create two monopolies, one being either Connecticut or Virginia, take the lighter monopoly if neither monopoly has reached the 50-50 point.

A ROLE FOR BALTIC TOO

The Baltic monopoly is not ordinarily a killer monopoly because it does not pull in enough rent to drive any opponent into bankruptcy. To win, the Baltic owner must not have any opponent with

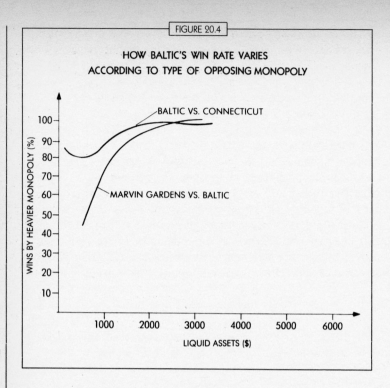

FIGURE 20.4

**HOW BALTIC'S WIN RATE VARIES
ACCORDING TO TYPE OF OPPOSING MONOPOLY**

a monopoly on the first two sides of the board or with over $1000 in liquid assets. Figure 20.4 illustrates how a Baltic monopoly owner can win if the strongest opponent owns the Marvin Gardens monopoly.

DEFEAT YOUR OPPONENT WITH GENEROSITY

Figure 20.4 points out a situation that arises every time your net liquid assets put you on the low side of the 50-50 point. If it is in your interest to take the cheaper monopoly, the more expensive the monopoly that you can get your opponent to take, the better is your probability of winning. For example, in Figure 20.4, you can almost double your chances of winning with Baltic by giving your opponent Marvin Gardens instead of Connecticut.

✻ STRATEGIC ADVANTAGE **63:** When it is in your interest to take a lighter monopoly, give your opponent the heaviest monopoly he or she will accept. While appearing to be generous (thus enabling you to demand additional "goodies" from your opponent as part of the trade), you actually increase the probability of choking your opponent into bankruptcy.

The idea applies in reverse when you have the heavier monopoly: give your opponent the cheapest monopoly he or she will accept. Whenever you get a monopoly that fits your own level of liquid assets, give your opponent a monopoly as far away as possible from your own monopoly. Give yourself maximum elbow room.

However, this advice is hard to follow when you have a heavy monopoly. Your opponents will resist taking a monopoly very much lighter than yours. In this case you cannot disguise giving yourself maximum elbow room as a gesture of generosity.

THE TIME IT TAKES TO WIN

It is helpful to know how long it takes to win because it helps identify whether you should play aggressively or conservatively.

Figure 20.5 shows a familiar checkmark curve along with a second curve, the time curve. The time curve shows how much time it took after the monopolies were created for the winner to win. (It was assumed players took one hour to move 150 times.)

The pattern shown in Figure 20.5 is true for all monopolies. When the lighter monopoly wins, it wins quickly. When the heavier monopoly wins, it takes longer.

If you own a light monopoly, you face a do-or-die situation. You must choke your opponents into bankruptcy quickly.

✻ STRATEGIC ADVANTAGE **64:** If you own a light monopoly, you must play aggressively so that the game will be over soon. Mortgage deeply, develop monopoly properties quickly, demortgage fast.

✻ STRATEGIC ADVANTAGE **65:** If you own a heavier monopoly, you should play conservatively. Do not take risks. Play to survive. The longer you survive, the more likely your monopoly is to become fully developed and bring you a win.

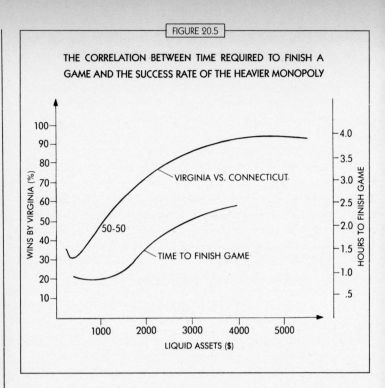

FIGURE 20.5

THE CORRELATION BETWEEN TIME REQUIRED TO FINISH A
GAME AND THE SUCCESS RATE OF THE HEAVIER MONOPOLY

* STRATEGIC ADVANTAGE 66: If you know an opponent is by
nature an aggressive risk taker, get that player to take a heavy
monopoly. Give conservative opponents light monopolies.
Such match-ups tend to cause your opponents to misplay the
game.

HOW TO PLAY THE WEAK SISTERS

Three killer monopolies, Virginia, Boardwalk, and Marvin Gardens,
always tend to lose to their neighbor on the same side of the board.
This does not mean that you cannot use Boardwalk or a weak sister
to win the game. A weak sister can still be the best monopoly on
the board—provided the stronger sister is not monopolized.

* STRATEGIC ADVANTAGE 67: Do not eliminate the weak sisters from your list of potential monopolies simply because they are weak sisters. They can win you the game if a weak sister's strong sister is not monopolized.

A weak sister is always weak only when matched against the stronger sister and is not necessarily weak against other monopolies.

Sometimes your only alternative to a weak sister is no monopoly at all. It is far better to accept the weak sister, as your sole prospect to win without a monopoly is to take over the monopoly of a bankrupt player late in the game. Your probability of winning with this strategy is, at best, 1 in 400; usually your chances of winning are less than 1 in 1000. Your chances are up to hundreds of times better by monopolizing the weak sister.

THE EIGHT-MONOPOLY TOURNAMENT: MULTIPLE MONOPOLIES

Most Monopoly games involve more than two players. Consequently, your monopoly must defeat more than one monopoly at a time if you are to win the game.

To discover if the three-house rule and the hotel rule can be used when many monopolies share the board, observe the results of a second set of tournament games. This tournament involved eight players, each of which owned one and only one of the eight monopolies. Various steps were taken to assure that the only significant factor affecting the outcomes of these games was the strength of each player's monopoly. The tournament consisted of 14,145 games. Each of these games would have lasted as long as 6⅓ hours if played by human players.

Before examining the results, some explanation is necessary. In an eight-player game, if all things were equal, each player would win one-eighth of the games played. Since you are presumably more interested in winning than in losing, Figure 20.6 shows only monopolies that won more than one-eighth of the games. It is thus a graph of how much better each monopoly performed percentage-wise than a monopoly that won exactly one-eighth of the games played. The graph shows monopolies' winning percentages according to the liquid assets existing when the monopolies were formed.

At early stages of the game, the Connecticut monopoly domi-

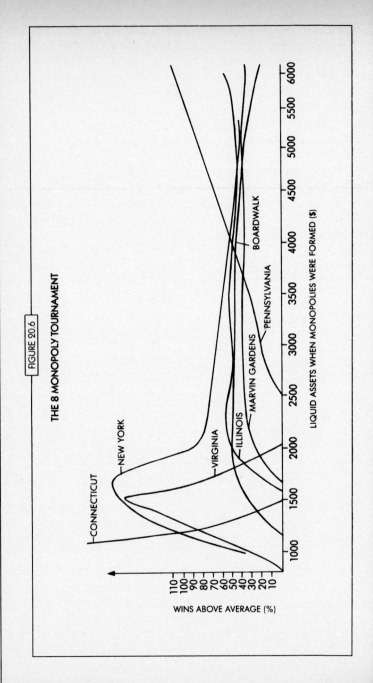

FIGURE 20.6

THE 8 MONOPOLY TOURNAMENT

CONNECTICUT

NEW YORK

VIRGINIA

ILLINOIS

MARVIN GARDENS

PENNSYLVANIA

BOARDWALK

WINS ABOVE AVERAGE (%)

LIQUID ASSETS WHEN MONOPOLIES WERE FORMED ($)

nates. Virginia and New York dominate after Connecticut fades. In succession, Boardwalk, then Illinois, then Marvin Gardens, and finally Pennsylvania join the parade of better-than-average monopolies as liquid assets increase. This is just as would be expected from the results of the one-on-one tournament.

Unfortunately, at higher liquid-asset levels, say above $2500, all the upper-tier monopolies perform nearly the same. There is very little difference in the winning percentage of New York, Boardwalk, Illinois, and the other upper-tier monopolies. The graph tells you that the principal difference between one upper-tier monopoly and another, when liquid assets are above $2500, is the luck of its owner! Furthermore, the hotel rule cannot be used to predict which of a pair of monopolies is better; instead use the rules in Strategic Advantages 68 and 69.

* **STRATEGIC ADVANTAGE 68:** If all players have or will have monopolies and if you have no more than $4000 in liquid assets, try to get either the New York (preferably) or Illinois monopoly.

* **STRATEGIC ADVANTAGE 69:** If all players have or will have monopolies and if you have over $4000 in liquid assets, try to get either the Pennsylvania (preferably) or Illinois monopoly.

You may recall that $4000 is the amount of money the bank feeds into the game for the players to share each hour.

GAMES WITH FEWER PLAYERS

Although the discussion to this point in the chapter has been based on eight-player, eight-monopoly games, the same lessons have been proved to apply with games with fewer players.

The Effect of Players without Monopolies

In the eight-monopoly tournament, all players had monopolies. Does it make a difference if there remain one or more players who do not own a monopoly after the monopoly chain reaction?

Several thousand experimental games were run in which one, two, or four of the players gained no monopoly during the monopoly chain reaction. The difference between games in which all players had monopolies and games in which one or more players remained monopolyless was striking.

One difference, which is not surprising, is that monopolyless players lose virtually all the games, and this increases the winning probabilities of every player who did own a monopoly.

The other difference is truly surprising and is a result few Monopoly players appreciate. The existence of players without monopolies weakens the New York and Boardwalk monopolies and reestablishes the validity of the hotel rule between upper-tier monopolies.

This means that if there is at least one player in the game who does not own a killer monopoly, you can use the hotel rule described earlier in this chapter (Strategic Advantage 58) to gain a significant advantage over opponents owning upper-tier monopolies.

> * **STRATEGIC ADVANTAGE 70:** If there is at least one monopolyless player in a multiplayer game, evaluate the relative value of upper-tier monopolies using the hotel rule (Strategic Advantage 58).

Why Do Monopolyless Players Affect the Relative Value of Monopolies?

The effect of monopolyless players is this: monopolyless players bring their cash flow into the game, but because they cannot extract much money from opposing players, their cash flow winds up in the hands of opposing players with monopolies. This benefits heavy-monopoly owners more than lower-tier monopoly owners, as lower-tier owners cannot invest extra cash they get as upper-tier owners can.

Whether or not there are monopolyless players makes no difference when liquid assets are low. The three-house rule always remains valid.

The effect of monopolyless players gives rise to one of the most interesting strategic maneuvers in any part of the game: If opponents own hotels on Pennsylvania, Marvin Gardens, or Illinois and you own Boardwalk or New York, give a monopolyless player a monopoly and you increase the winning chances of the New York and Boardwalk monopolies.

✳ **STRATEGIC ADVANTAGE 71:** In a game with many upper-tier hotels, give monopolyless players a monopoly to strengthen the winning power of the Boardwalk and New York monopolies.

TRADES FOR MONOPOLIES BETWEEN UNEQUAL PLAYERS

All the statistics in this chapter have come from games whose players had equal liquid assets. One reason the three-house rule and the hotel rule are so useful is that you can use them even if the trading players do not have equal liquid assets.

If you are wealthier than your trading partner, you can apply the three-house rule and the hotel rule just as for equally wealthy players. For every potential trade with a poorer player, you simply reach the 50-50 point earlier.

If You Are the Poorer Player

When you have lower liquid assets than the player with whom you wish to trade, the hotel and three-house rules can be used, but you must use the liquid assets of the richer player to judge which of a pair of monopolies is better for that player and then, of course, propose that he or she take the other monopoly.

✳ **STRATEGIC ADVANTAGE 72:** When evaluating a trade with a wealthier player, use the three-house or hotel rule, using your opponent's liquid assets as the basis.

As a general rule, it is in your interest to give your opponent the lighter monopoly. It is nearly impossible for a poorer player with a lighter monopoly to defeat a wealthier player who has reached the 50-50 point. This illustrates the need for poor players to arrange trades early in the game. This is another reason that you should get into the habit of using the I2 predictor.

21 🚂

Strategic Trading

Strategic trading means trading for a monopoly. The best trades are not necessarily easy to see, so you must prepare for strategic trades before all the properties have been sold or auctioned.

Simply getting a clear idea of who owns what is vital. Some familiarity with all players' property holdings comes naturally as the game progresses, but it is advantageous to have a closer familiarity with property ownership than your opponents. Some players devote nearly all their attention to happenings on the gameboard and hardly any attention to the Title Deed cards in front of each player.

✳ STRATEGIC ADVANTAGE 73: Get into the habit of studying the ownership of color groups. When an opponent lands on another opponent's property, study the ownership of all the properties on that color group during the free time you have while opponents exchange rent money.

Most of the unexpected, creative deals seem to be proposed by players who have the ownership of all properties well established in their minds. You can use this generalization to predict which players are likely to propose nonobvious trades and which players will not.

∗ **STRATEGIC ADVANTAGE 74:** Take note of which players miss rents due them or otherwise have difficulty identifying who owns a property after a landing. You can usually count on such players to recognize and propose only the most obvious trades, if any at all. The opposite type of player presents a danger to your own strategic plans.

One important reason to be prepared is so that you can immediately offer counterproposals. If a player with whom you were intending to trade receives first a trade offer from yet another opponent, you have less than a minute to decide what to do. If unprepared, you are liable to do no better than to complain, "Aw, you'd be crazy to take that deal!"

WINDOWS FOR SUCCESS

In 1980s parlance, a "window" refers to the period of time during which a spacecraft must blast off if it is going to blast off at all and avoid a scrubbed mission. Windows exist for monopolies too. The best monopoly for you changes as playing time and liquid assets increase. You have a limited period of time during which you must gain ownership of a particular killer monopoly to gain maximum benefit. If you fail to get a monopoly during its window, your best chance of winning is likely to be the next available heavier monopoly.

Effective negotiating may require considerable time and, very possibly, more than one "negotiating session." If you and your opponents continue to circuit the board and to increase your liquid assets while you negotiate, you may be pulled out of your window for success.

To prevent this, you should start negotiating for a monopoly near the beginning, or possibly before the beginning, of its window.

∗ **STRATEGIC ADVANTAGE 75:** Start negotiations for a particular monopoly while your liquid assets are still short of the ideal amount in order to allow sufficient negotiating time.

Windows are a greater problem when your goal is the lighter of a pair of monopolies. The longer a trade is delayed, the better are the chances of success for the heavier monopoly. Therefore, stalling and delay are tactics best suited for the player aiming for heavier monopoly. The player acquiring the lighter monopoly has a time deadline to meet.

ACCEPT A TRADE IN REVERSE

If you are offered a light monopoly when your liquid assets would support the heavier monopoly your opponent wants you to trade away, try to reverse the trade. Ask if your opponent really thinks the trade will benefit both sides. Of course, he or she will answer yes. Having obtained agreement that the trade is good for both sides, point out that it is logical that he or she should be willing to accept the equally desirable lighter monopoly. Seldom will an opponent agree to do the trade exactly in reverse, but you will nevertheless have established a basis for negotiating in that direction.

> ∗ **STRATEGIC ADVANTAGE 76:** When you are offered a monopoly-forming trade that is far from ideal, commit your trading partner to an even deal. Then reverse the trade.

HOW TO IDENTIFY AND EVALUATE YOUR TRADING ALTERNATIVES

All monopoly trades can be classified as one of three types: simple swaps, compound deals, and group trades.

Simple Swaps

Never unnoticed by any player are potential trades that require only a simple swap. The situation in Figure 21.1, which is a diagram of two three-lot color groups owned by Players A and B, is typical for simple swaps. (Figure 21.1 could, for example, represent the Illinois and Marvin Gardens monopolies when Player A owns Kentucky and Indiana and Player B owns Illinois Avenue and when they also share ownership of the Marvin Gardens lots.)

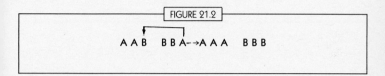

FIGURE 21.1

A A B   B B A

A swap of one property for another results in two new monopolies, as in Figure 21.2.

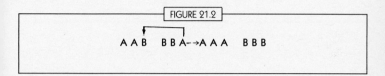

FIGURE 21.2

A A B   B B A→A A A   B B B

The notation used in Figure 21.2 means that Player A proposed a trade to Player B, whereby Player A gave up ownership of the lot at one end of the solid arrow in exchange for the lot at the other end. This resulted in a monopoly for each player as shown by the ownership diagram to the right of the broken arrow.

A lucky player may have more than one simple-swap monopoly-forming opportunity, as in Figure 21.3. In this case, a deeper evaluation is necessary.

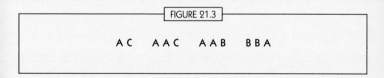

FIGURE 21.3

A C   A A C   A A B   B B A

Player A has simple swap possibilities with both opponents, B and C. If Player A proposes a simple swap with Player B, the result will be as shown in Figure 21.4.

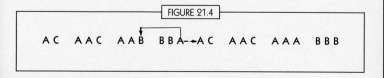

FIGURE 21.4

A C   A A C   A A B   B B A→A C   A A C   A A A   B B B

Assuming that AC is the Baltic color group, Player B should realize that the three-lot monopoly he can offer Player A is better than what Player A can get from Player C. Player B thus has some bargaining power. Player B should demand that Player A also give or sell (or offer an option for) a property that would make it impossible for Player A later to form a second monopoly with Player C. The deal that Player B should propose is diagrammed in Figure 21.5.

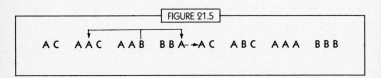

FIGURE 21.5

AC AAC AAB BBA→AC ABC AAA BBB

Any deal that results in a monopoly is met with not only hope but also with a sense of relief. Whenever you agree to a trade giving an opponent a killer monopoly, do not underestimate your bargaining power. Do not hesitate to look beyond the immediate trade. Demand additional concessions concerning the possibilities of your opponent's gaining additional monopolies in the future.

Behavioral psychologists have proved that in balancing the rewards and consequences of our actions, guaranteed benefits here and now greatly outweigh uncertain benefits in the future.

＊STRATEGIC ADVANTAGE 77: When giving an opponent a certain benefit (such as a monopoly) right away, demand a concession that takes place in the future whose penalties are uncertain. When giving a player a monopoly-forming property, demand additional properties that block future monopolies.

In the example of Figure 21.3, Player A could have first proposed a trade with Player C, as in Figure 21.6, thus leaving Player B unable to demand an additional concession. Diplomats call such a maneuver a fait accompli.

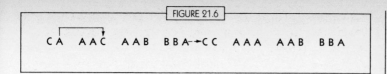

FIGURE 21.6

C A   A A C   A A B   B B A→C C   A A A   A A B   B B A

Whether it would be wise for Player A to do this depends on Player B's alternatives elsewhere on the board. If Player B has no other reasonable chance for a monopoly, Player B is likely to accept a no-strings-attached trade with Player A, as shown in Figure 21.7.

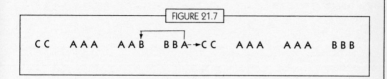

FIGURE 21.7

C C   A A A   A A B   B B A→C C   A A A   A A A   B B B

Player A thus leaves this sequence of trades with two monopolies rather than one.

This example illustrates one of the reasons that the number of alternative monopoly trades is the greatest single source of power and success in Monopoly and why you should identify all possible alternatives you and each of your opponents have to form a monopoly. (It will be explained later why you should avoid trading with a player who has more alternatives than you.)

It may seem sensible to try to trade for lots that increase your trade alternatives. Unfortunately, in single-swap situations, all players realize why you are trying to get the property you are trying to get. They will therefore put a high price on such a property.

Trading for properties that block an opponent's existing alternatives is generally more successful because it is not apparent to all players exactly what you are doing. Furthermore, if the owner of such a property already has a killer monopoly, that player is generally preoccupied with gaining cash to build that monopoly.

✳ **STRATEGIC ADVANTAGE 78:** Use simple swaps to reduce an opponent's monopoly-forming trade alternatives rather than to attempt to increase your own trade alternatives.

✳ **STRATEGIC ADVANTAGE 79:** If you have only one trade possibility to form a monopoly, trade with others to narrow your trading partner's alternatives down to only yourself.

Compound Swaps

Sometimes you must consider more complicated deals to widen your alternatives. Figure 21.8 is an example of a compound swap, a less obvious trade opportunity.

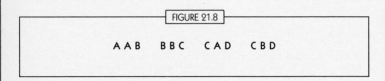

FIGURE 21.8

A A B   B B C   C A D   C B D

Either Player A or Player B must induce Player C to give up the third lot of the second color group to enable Players A and B to form monopolies. However, there is no way for Player A to reward Player C for cooperating. Player C would be left with no additional monopoly opportunities (as shown in Figure 21.9) while creating one for Players A and B.

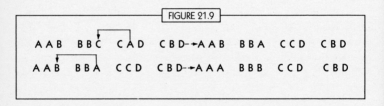

FIGURE 21.9

A A B   B B C   C A D   C B D→A A B   B B A   C C D   C B D
A A B   B B A   C C D   C B D→A A A   B B B   C C D   C B D

Player B must provide an incentive for Players A and C to trade by selling Player C a property, as illustrated in Figure 21.10.

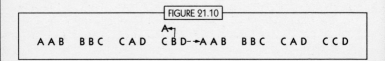

FIGURE 21.10

A A B   B B C   C A D   C B D→A A B   B B C   C A D   C C D

Once this trade is completed, it is in Player C's interest to allow Players A and B to share a monopoly opportunity, as Player C gains a possible deal with Player D (see Figure 21.11).

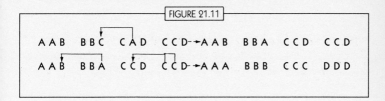

FIGURE 21.11

If you are Player A in the situation in Figure 21.11, you are powerless to act unless Player B acts first. Do not hesitate to point out to an opponent the trade possibilities with a third player. Your potential trading partner may not have recognized it.

✳ **STRATEGIC ADVANTAGE 80:** Grease the way for a compound swap by creating opportunities for opponents to trade with you, and do not hesitate to point out compound swaps with your potential trading partner. That player may have failed to act through simple oversight.

Group Trades

Group trades, fortunately, are easier to recognize than compound swaps. Group trades involve three or more players who simultaneously each gain one monopoly.

Suppose that you are Player A in Figure 21.12.

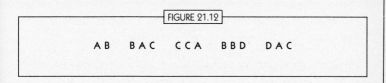

FIGURE 21.12

Suppose also that you hope soon to gain ownership of the first three-lot monopoly, which you share with Players B and C. Accomplishing that with a sequence of compound swaps would be difficult, if not impossible.

The solution is a group trade. You can recognize a group trade by counting the number of color groups that are exclusively owned by the same players. If the number of color groups equals or exceeds the number of identical players, a group trade is possible.

✻ **STRATEGIC ADVANTAGE 81:** Identify group trades by counting the number of color groups controlled by a given number of players. If the number of color groups equals or exceeds the number of players, a group trade possibility exists.

Figure 21.12 is an example of how a group trade can be used advantageously. Players A, B, and C (three players) have exclusive control over three color groups, A B, B A C, and C C A. The resulting monopolies of a three-player group trade can be divided among the players six ways; the limiting factor is what is acceptable to all the players involved.

In the present example, one way to divide the monopolies is shown in Figure 21.13.

FIGURE 21.13

B B   A A A   C C C   B B D   D A C

A four-player group trade is also possible in the present example, but it is usually to your advantage to minimize the number of players involved. First, the greater the number of players involved, the greater the possibility of a conflict that will prevent the deal from taking place. Each participant in a group deal has veto power. Second, the fewer the number of players, the fewer the number of manufactured monopolies that you must defeat.

✻ **STRATEGIC ADVANTAGE 82:** When assembling group trade possibilities, minimize the number of players involved.

There is a major exception to this advice. If a pair of opponents can with a simple swap form strong monopolies, you should consider including one or both of the players in a group deal so that their swap becomes impossible or at least less likely.

Be the player who proposes a group deal. If you design the trade, you can propose one in which you gain the monopoly you want.

Also important, if you are the proposer, you can select the way to equalize the deal. There usually must be a provision to equalize what each player gets out of the deal in relation to what each puts in. Otherwise, one of the players is liable to veto the trade.

Besides not equalizing the deal at all, your choices as the group trade designer are to equalize properties or to equalize cash.

Cash equalization means that every player is credited with an amount equal to the face value of the property given away and is charged an amount equal to the face value of properties gained. The player collects or pays the difference.

Property equalization means that players who leave a deal with fewer properties than they had before the trade must be compensated by the players who increased their number of properties through the trade. Properties offered as compensation may come from lots in parts of the board not monopolized.

If you will leave a group trade with one of the cheaper monopolies, it is usually in your interest to have the property exchanges equalized by cash because you thus receive cash at a stage in the game when ordinary properties are worth little.

＊STRATEGIC ADVANTAGE 83: Take the initiative to be the proposer of group trades.

＊STRATEGIC ADVANTAGE 84: Equalize group trades with cash if you leave the trade with a lighter monopoly.

If you are going to come out of the trade having gained more expensive properties than you surrendered, it is in your interest to equalize the trade with equivalent properties.

＊STRATEGIC ADVANTAGE 85: If you leave a group trade with a heavier monopoly, equalize the trade with equivalent ordinary properties or propose that the deal not be equalized. This prevents you from losing cash when cash is all-important.

CONSIDER GROUP TRADES EARLY IN THE GAME

Many players never independently consider the possibilities of a group trade. This gives you an opportunity to improve your bargaining power. You should use this opportunity even if you have good prospects for a desirable monopoly-forming simple swap.

Announce to opponents the possibilities of a group trade, even if you secretly do not want it to succeed. Such an announcement shows to all opponents that you have an additional monopoly-forming alternative besides your obvious single-swap trade.

TRADING AFTER THE BIG TRADE

The most critical trade is, of course, the trade for your initial monopoly. Seldom does it pay to take a "bad" first monopoly with the hope of acquiring a better monopoly afterward.

This does not mean that you should ignore other monopoly trade possibilities after you have gained ownership of a suitable monopoly. (The issues to think about concerning additional trades were detailed in Chapter 17.)

22

Effective Negotiating Techniques

Having learned to distinguish diamonds from glass, you cannot expect automatically to be swimming in diamonds. So it is in Monopoly. Knowing exactly which monopolies can win you the game is one thing; gaining ownership of them is another. Gaining ownership of a winning monopoly usually means that you must put together deals or trades with your opponents; that is, you must negotiate!

Until recent times common opinion was that the ability to negotiate demanded an outgoing personality, quick wits, and an even quicker tongue. Now researchers have proved that there is a pattern to successful negotiating. This pattern can be learned. Do what expert negotiators do and you are guaranteed to negotiate more successfully. You will especially benefit from learning these techniques if negotiating is not part of your daily life.

Compared to other cultures, there is little opportunity to practice negotiating in the United States. This may explain why most world champion Monopoly players in recent years have been foreigners.

STYLES OF NEGOTIATING

All recent books about negotiating describe a style of negotiating called the win-win style. Before describing win-win negotiating, it will be helpful to consider the older major style, which may be called win-lose negotiating or verbal bullying. The purpose of describing it is not to persuade you to use it but to assure that you can deal with it.

The Verbal Bully

Verbal bullying is characterized by anger, loud voices, table pounding, caustic remarks, and a combination of extreme behaviors: shouting and silence, laughter and crying, and anxiety and friendliness. This kind of negotiator tries to force you to make a decision based on emotion or feelings rather than on thought.

The verbal bully may seem to have lost self-control but probably has not. You may recall the blustery United Nations speech by Soviet Premier Khrushchev in which he threatened, while pounding his shoe on the podium, to bury us. Most people believe he simply lost his composure and thus came to use such blunt language unintentionally. Almost unnoticed was the fact that while Khrushchev was pounding the shoe on the podium, he was wearing two shoes. He had apparently planned ahead by bringing an extra shoe!

When facing a verbal bully, remember that if you feel threatened, embarrassed, or weary and in need of peace, you are feeling exactly how your negotiating partner wants you to feel. Accepting the bully's deal may give you temporary peace, but you are likely to regret it in the long run.

DEALING WITH THE BULLY

How should you handle the verbal bully? You should not say to go away and bother somebody else if he or she has something of value to you.

The best way to defuse the situation is to expose the verbal bully's negotiating tactics. An exposed negotiating ploy is an ineffective ploy.

＊**STRATEGIC ADVANTAGE 86:** Neutralize the verbal bully by remaining calm and by exposing the emotion-laden, intimidating tactics the bully is using.

A simple, effective response to the bully is, "I can hear you talk louder and louder, but your offer is as weak as it ever was. Instead of talking louder, why don't you concentrate on making a reasonable offer?"

Win-Win Negotiating

One good reason to use win-win negotiation techniques is that they are more pleasant. Another is that they are usually more effective.

Not everyone is an intellectual giant, yet all humans seem to retain a mental sharpness for preserving their own self-interest. People think extra hard when they sense that their own well-being is at stake. Win-win negotiating is a way of negotiating that recognizes that everyone is sharp in matters of self-interest.

No Monopoly player will purposely hurt his or her own chances of winning by helping you to win. Win-win negotiating recognizes that you must offer something that at least appears to improve your negotiating partner's chances to win if you are going to get something of value in return.

WIN-WIN NEGOTIATIONS. TYPICAL MONOPOLY NEGOTIATIONS

Here is a typical Monopoly bargaining exchange.

"Listen, Joe, I'll give you $300 for New York Avenue."

"That's not enough; New York would give you a chance for a monopoly. I won't sell it for under $900."

"C'mon, Joe, get serious. I'll give you $500 and no more. That monopoly is not a sure thing."

"I'll split the difference with you. Give me $700 and it's yours."

"I've already raised my offer; $600 is final."

"Okay, it's yours for $600."

The process starts with each side announcing its "price." To each side the price is a solution to a problem—possibly to two different problems.

Although this kind of bargaining may result in an agreement, it is unlikely that either side benefited as much as it could have. That is, the total benefits the bargainers gained was probably suboptimal.

AVOID SUBOPTIMAL TRADES

In Monopoly there is a major problem with suboptimal trades. You need to defeat more than just one player. Getting the best of an opponent in a trading deal is not the point of the game. You need to gain enough from a trade to defeat *all* players.

Win-win negotiating is an effort to optimize the benefits to both sides. It is a bargaining method whose goal is to give each side more of what it truly needs. Therefore, the negotiators put more distance between themselves and the remaining players.

This does not mean that neither side gets the better of the other in a deal. While both sides may win more, it remains likely that one side will win more than the other. The important point is that both sides gain ground on the other players in the game.

STARTING A WIN-WIN NEGOTIATION

The key idea behind win-win negotiation is *not* to jump immediately into back-and-forth price bargaining. Instead, take each negotiation through two stages: (1) gather information about the opposing side's perceived needs and (2) gain agreements.

> ∗ **STRATEGIC ADVANTAGE 87:** Resist the tendency to state your demands immediately. Follow a two-stage process in every negotiation. Only after gaining information from your opponent should you begin to exchange demands.

What is the big advantage of the two-stage process? Researchers have found that estimating the real goals of the other side is what negotiators do most poorly. Figuring out the other side's needs is where there is most room for improvement. The two-stage process forces you to concentrate energy and time in this area.

In short, win-win negotiating requires that you ask questions before you state your demands. Negotiating experts suggest that during stage 1 you should apply Strategic Advantages 87 through 91.

> ∗ **STRATEGIC ADVANTAGE 88:** Make your negotiating partner agree that there is a need for an agreement. That is, get your opponent to agree that there is something to be gained for both sides.

> ∗ **STRATEGIC ADVANTAGE 89:** Avoid arguments—even if the other side argues. If your opponent says something you can-

not accept, do not immediately express your own view. First, say in a personal way that you understand what your opponent says or why he or she says it. Only then should you counter with your own opinion.

✳ STRATEGIC ADVANTAGE 90: Do not act as if you can immediately see the impact of your opponent's proposal, even if you do. Instead, ask questions. Get your negotiating partner to explain the benefits of the proposal to both sides.

✳ STRATEGIC ADVANTAGE 91: Do not debate the fairness or rightness of each other's demands. Debate the *results*.

✳ STRATEGIC ADVANTAGE 92: Listening carefully, ferret out your negotiating partner's main concerns. What is your opponent really aiming for? Why is your opponent reluctant to do what you want him or her to do?

After you fully understand your partner's viewpoints and goals, you will more likely be able to make an offer he or she can accept, and you should go on to the second stage to cement a deal. Strategic Advantages 92 through 101 provide guidelines to follow during the second stage.

✳ STRATEGIC ADVANTAGE 93: If you cannot reach agreement, divide your proposal into smaller pieces and try to get an agreement on one of the segments. Even small agreements create momentum that can help solve the truly important issue.

✳ STRATEGIC ADVANTAGE 94: Be persistent and keep dialogue alive. The more time and effort your partner puts into the negotiation, the more compelled he or she feels to make something come of it.

✳ STRATEGIC ADVANTAGE 95: Make all your offers with the idea that it may not be the last offer you will have to make. Inflate your demands to allow room for additional compromise.

✳ STRATEGIC ADVANTAGE 96: Appear reluctant to accept any offer—even if it is just what you had been waiting for. Grimace, wrinkle your nose, or skew your face upon receiving any offer. Never accept the first offer.

✷ STRATEGIC ADVANTAGE **97:** Do not offer your first compromise until your partner has compromised once. In other words, compromise last.

✷ STRATEGIC ADVANTAGE **98:** Let your partner make the offer to split the difference. That leaves you the option of treating the split as being the present offer, and you can try to get a still better deal.

✷ STRATEGIC ADVANTAGE **99:** Demand a concession for every concession you make.

✷ STRATEGIC ADVANTAGE **100:** Make fewer offers than your opponent. If he or she says, "You'll have to do better than that," do not make a new offer. Instead ask, "How much better?"

✷ STRATEGIC ADVANTAGE **101:** Shift your problems to the other side. That is, if your opponent says, "You don't have enough cash to throw into the deal," you can respond, "Well, what do you think can be done about that?"

✷ STRATEGIC ADVANTAGE **102:** Consider the effect of the size of your concessions. If your concessions are too small, your partner may believe that you are not serious about reaching an agreement. If you concede too much, your partner may expect greater concessions in the future than you are willing to make.

ASPIRATION LEVEL

Aspiration level refers to a negotiator's expectations or goals. For example, when buying a new car, your aspiration level is the discount below sticker price the dealer must offer to win your business. Recent studies have proved that success in negotiating depends more on aspiration level than on anything else.

The clear lesson from these studies is always to aim high. A suitable goal for any strategic deal in Monopoly is to get a good killer monopoly while leaving you enough cash and unmortgaged property to win.

> ✳ STRATEGIC ADVANTAGE 103: Aim to leave any monopoly-creating trade with a monopoly on the best side of the board and with enough liquid assets to develop that monopoly fully.

Creating high aspirations for yourself is not as simple as it sounds. Setting higher aspirations means that you set a higher standard for yourself to have success, which in turn means that you have to accept a greater risk of failure.

If you know the game better than your opponents, your superior Monopoly skills can actually make setting high goals more difficult. You may recognize your strategic weaknesses while your opponents may not recognize theirs. It can be easier for unskilled players to maintain high aspirations.

At the same time you try to maximize your own aspirations, you must try to lower those of your opponents.

> ✳ STRATEGIC ADVANTAGE 104: Everything you do during a negotiation should be done with the idea of lowering your negotiating partners' aspirations.

There are three ways to lower opponents' aspirations: use knowledge, use time, and use power. All negotiations should be conducted with the idea of managing all three to lower the other side's aspirations. The combination of knowledge, time, and power is what is commonly called "bargaining power."

MANAGING KNOWLEDGE

Do not assume that your negotiating partners share your beliefs about which properties and monopolies are most valuable. All players have had different experiences and thus have developed differing viewpoints of any game situation.

Past experiences cause players to overvalue some properties and undervalue others. Discovering your opponents' opinions of the value of particular properties is an important winning advantage. The best deals are those in which you gain a winning-quality monopoly while giving an opponent a monopoly that he or she believes is strong but is actually weak.

* **STRATEGIC ADVANTAGE 105:** During stage 1 of negotiations, uncover opponents' beliefs and opinions about the values of monopoly properties. Try to not reveal your own opinions.

In a negotiation, few people will tell you much unless you reciprocate by revealing some of your own thoughts. It is useful to adopt a "public face" about the relative values of monopoly properties to hide your own opinions. A particularly effective public face is that the value of a property is proportional to its cost. Most players believe this to be true, so this is a credible posture.

* **STRATEGIC ADVANTAGE 106:** Adopt a public face that the winning strength of a monopoly is proportional to its cost.

New Information

One trait of effective negotiators is that they use "new information." In Monopoly new information comes from recognizing change. Change occurs as the various monopolies gain and lose power and advantage. Bring your knowledge of these changes into negotiations by using new information to justify or show evidence for not improving your latest offer or even for lowering your offer. Introducing new information can confuse or panic opponents, leading them to accept your proposal quickly.

* **STRATEGIC ADVANTAGE 107:** Use your knowledge of changes in the strength of various players and of the changes of monopoly values to justify or show evidence for your negotiating position. Use new information to create confusion or panic.

MANAGING TIME

A shortage of time or a deadline creates pressure to agree. Everyone who has written about negotiating has noted how willing people are to accept deadlines imposed by others. This is true for false deadlines as well as for real ones. Therefore, you can use deadlines to pressure opponents into an agreement quickly.

> ✳ STRATEGIC ADVANTAGE 108: When negotiating, set the deadlines yourself, and do not hesitate to set deadlines for your opponents.

When a deadline is forced on you, act as if you are not concerned about time. Of course, you usually do have a deadline in the back of your mind when negotiating for a monopoly. You must try to keep it a secret.

Short deadlines are usually needed for the lighter monopolies. Long deadlines or no deadlines are generally best when you are trying to assemble a heavy monopoly.

To lend credibility to a demand for a short deadline, you should try to introduce new information about changes in the game, as new information makes the use of a deadline more effective.

MANAGING POWER

Power is the ability to persuade an opponent to do what you want him or her to do. Power is leverage. The more powerful an opponent considers you to be, the more inclined he or she will be to do what you ask. Negotiating power is the subject of the old joke that a smile and a gun will get you more than a smile alone.

Unlike competitors in most other games, almost every Monopoly player has during at least part of the game a great deal of power. No Monopoly player can be treated lightly or ignored, because every player has the potential power to trip you up on your way to a win. Though this may be uncomfortable when you are on top and running strong, it is a source of strength and optimism when your luck has been bad and it is difficult to see any path toward victory.

What Determines Power in Monopoly?

The most important factor determining power in Monopoly is the power to reward. The more players you can reward with valuable properties (properties leading to monopolies), the more power you have. In some games the ability to enrich a player through an additional Railroad or Utility is also important. The ability to reward opponents is a gold mine for yourself, because you have the ability to demand value-adding properties in return.

* **STRATEGIC ADVANTAGE 109:** Trade for properties that increase your opportunities to reward opponents.

The second most important power factor is competition to your ability to reward. The greater the number of players you can reward, the greater power you can assert over any particular player. In short, the more alternatives you have to make deals, the more power you have.

* **STRATEGIC ADVANTAGE 110:** Trade for properties that increase your alternatives to reward opponents.

Any time you have the power to reward, you also have the power to punish. You have the power to punish all players through your ability to make any one player stronger. Even if you cannot offer any player a killer monopoly, you may still have power to punish by being able to tip the balance in any particular player's direction. The power to punish is why it is rare for any Monopoly player to be completely powerless. The disadvantage of this kind of power is that it sometimes means punishing yourself, as exercising this type of power jeopardizes (at least temporarily) your chances to win. For this reason the power to punish is better used as a threat than as an act.

* **STRATEGIC ADVANTAGE 111:** Use your power to punish when you have little power to reward or few trading alternatives.

Group Identification Power

People tend to empathize and cooperate with people with whom they share similar circumstances. Monopoly often turns into a game of "haves" versus "have-nots." If you are a have-not, you can find sympathetic ears by pointing out your common predicament to fellow have-not players.

* **STRATEGIC ADVANTAGE 112:** When you are poor or have no

good prospects for trades, identify other players in the same situation. Point out to them your common situation to stimulate them to be more receptive to trades

Wealth and Income

Greater wealth or income gives you a larger number of alternatives to win the game. That is, your selection of game-winning monopolies increases. There is a negative side to this power factor, however. Players might be afraid to trade with a wealthy opponent for fear that such a player may dominate the game after obtaining a monopoly. This is a realistic fear, so the "wealth disguises" described earlier can be a useful aim to winning when you have the happy problem of being very rich.

Real Power Is Perceived Power

For negotiating power to be useful, your opponents must see your power. Hidden power or power that negotiating partners simply do not notice does not help persuade opponents to your point of view. Therefore, you should make sure that any player with whom you negotiate fully appreciates the power you have in the game.

∗ **STRATEGIC ADVANTAGE 113:** Display your powers to reward. Display your powers to punish. Display your alternatives for trades.

The best way to "display" power is to open false negotiations. False negotiations are negotiations that you do not intend to carry through to agreement. For example, if you want to let Player A know that you can make a deal with Player B, you can simply ask if Player B is interested in trading a property for one of yours. This makes it very clear that you have an alternative to negotiating with Player A.

Do not give away any property that reduces your alternatives for a monopoly unless you get compensation. Demand a concession for anything that reduces your power to reward or punish or that reduces your trade alternatives.

WITH WHOM SHOULD YOU NEGOTIATE?

All else being equal, trade with the player who has the least power compared to yourself. Before you reach the monopoly chain reaction, estimate the bargaining power of each of your opponents by counting each of their trading alternatives.

> ✳ STRATEGIC ADVANTAGE 114: Estimate the bargaining power of each opponent by counting each opponent's monopoly trade alternatives. Aim to trade with a player who has less power than yourself.

PLOYS, MANEUVERS, AND GAMBITS

Professional diplomats and other expert negotiators have developed a number of tricks that have proved successful throughout the world. Several of these negotiation tricks are particularly useful for persuading Monopoly opponents to agree to your terms for trades.

> ✳ STRATEGIC ADVANTAGE 115: Consider using the "playing dumb" ploy.

When you want to sell an asset for more than it is really worth, you can simply "not understand" your opponent's explanations of why you are being unreasonable. Often, playing dumb can be best done by referring to real or imagined precedents. An example of a "dumb" precedent is, "Last time I played I sold Boardwalk for $800, so that is the lowest offer that I will accept." Playing dumb works best if your negotiating partner has no alternative for trades other than with you.

> ✳ STRATEGIC ADVANTAGE 116: Consider using the "withdraw offer" maneuver.

After trading demands back and forth for a while, you may find it useful simply to withdraw your previous best offer. This is best done on the basis of "new information" such as, "It's now plain to see that Player C is now richer than he was before, so your offer is not as valuable as it was before." This leaves your negotiating partner struggling to get you to remake an offer that he or she had previously rejected.

✻ STRATEGIC ADVANTAGE 117: Consider using the "red herring" gambit.

This gambit involves creating a false important issue. Suppose you are negotiating an important deal that would create two new killer monopolies. Into this discussion you could insert a demand that you also trade some Railroads. If after much negotiation you drop the demand for a Railroad trade, it would appear as if you made a major concession. Your opponent may thus be more inclined to accept your proposal on the more important issue of creating two new killer monopolies.

✻ STRATEGIC ADVANTAGE 118: Consider using the "one last bite" maneuver.

After negotiating an agreement important to both sides, your partner will be relieved finally to have reached agreement. (All negotiations create stress that neither side enjoys.) You can take advantage of your opponent's more relaxed frame of mind to take one little additional bite of his or her cash or property. It is likely that he or she will not be in a mood to start negotiating all over again and will therefore be inclined to give in a little bit more. For example, if you had agreed to trade New York for Kentucky, getting one last bite would be to demand $20 cash to make up for the difference in face value between the two properties.

✻ STRATEGIC ADVANTAGE 119: Consider using the "brinkmanship" maneuver.

This maneuver involves threatening to pull your negotiating partner (along with yourself and others) into certain defeat if you cannot reach an agreement. This maneuver requires that there be a third player whom you could reward with a very desirable property. It is necessary to be subtle when employing the brinkmanship maneuver. Do not simply threaten your negotiating partner. Instead, break off negotiations with your primary negotiation partner and start talking with the third player. Ask if the third player would be interested in a property that would almost certainly win that player the game. Discuss the property long enough with the third player that your primary negotiating partner appreciates what would happen if your "deal" with the third player goes through. Then think of a reason or excuse to negotiate again with your primary negotiating partner. You will have greatly increased your negotiating power.

✳ **STRATEGIC ADVANTAGE 120:** Consider using the "forest fire" gambit.

This gambit involves giving an opponent a property that provides a killer monopoly while in return you gain properties that do not give you any monopoly at all. This gambit is useful when you have no good trade alternatives with any player, that is, when you essentially have no power except the power to punish. You should be able to extract from the player whom you rewarded with a monopoly some number of properties that are desired by your other opponents. This gambit increases your power by creating competition for your properties. To make this gambit work you must quickly negotiate subsequent deals with one of the remaining players who do not own a monopoly. The subsequent deals must be made quickly because otherwise the player with the monopoly will run away with the game. In other words, without a quick second trade you are liable to be burned by the forest fire you created.

This gambit works best when you choose the most unskilled player as the one to get the initial killer monopoly. You want skilled players to remain without a monopoly, as skilled players will more readily recognize the need for quick agreements. If there are too many unskilled players without a monopoly, it may take too much time for them to realize that they must also gain monopolies. They will be burned by your forest fire, but so will you!

✳ **STRATEGIC ADVANTAGE 121:** Consider using the "Chinese auction" maneuver.

This maneuver involves dealing at the same time with more than one opponent. The Chinese auction works only when you have more than one potential deal with different opponents. Although you may have a definite preference about which of the players can help you the most, you can play one opponent against another to force the player with whom you really want to deal to improve an offer. You must think of good reasons or excuses to switch your negotiating attention back and forth between opponents; otherwise, this maneuver is liable to be exposed.

* **STRATEGIC ADVANTAGE 122:** Consider the use of meaningless concessions.

Demand concessions for every concession you make, but make some of your concessions meaningless or valueless. Examples of meaningless concessions are throwing in a strategically unimportant mortgaged property into the deal or agreeing to keep on negotiating in exchange for the other side's concession. The ultimate meaningless concession is to give an irreversibly poor player a monopoly in exchange for properties that will strengthen your position.

* **STRATEGIC ADVANTAGE 123:** Consider using the "scoundrel" maneuver.

To use this maneuver you keep your negotiating partner so occupied with negotiating with you that he or she does not pay attention to other alternatives. When the other alternatives eventually disappear, you face an opponent with no alternatives except to negotiate with you, and this, of course, puts you in the advantageous power position.

* **STRATEGIC ADVANTAGE 124:** Consider the "ultimatum" ploy.

Announce to your opponent that you will make one final offer. If this is not accepted, there will be no deal. Ultimatums can succeed only if the negotiating partner has only poor alternatives. To make an ultimatum more likely to succeed, make the alternative public and threaten indefinite deadlock. This puts the stress of a time deadline on your opponent. You should be aware that if an ultimatum is not accepted and if you try to reopen the negotiation, your credibility is greatly decreased. Do not use an ultimatum unless you are reasonably sure it will succeed.

STRATEGIC ADVANTAGE 125: Consider using the "confusion" gambit.

Present complicated deals to opponents with little introduction and with minimal explanation. Press for quick agreement. Your aim with the confusion gambit is that all the ramifications of the deal will not be immediately seen. This gambit works best with three- or four-player deals because such deals are inherently more complicated and because individuals involved may be motivated not to ask questions for fear of appearing to be a dullard.

STRATEGIC ADVANTAGE 126: Consider using your power to declare a stalemate.

If you need a trade to be completed fast in order for it to be helpful to you, you can threaten to declare the game a tie or a stalemate. Tell your opponents that you have reached your "boredom limit" and that "it makes no sense to continue playing Monopoly with no monopolies." Make it clear that you are willing to end the game rather than to continue circling the board when there are no monopolies to make it interesting.

Youngsters use a variation of this ploy, when they threaten their playmates to take their ball and go home. Just as youngsters cannot use this ploy if someone else has a ball, you cannot use it when any other player has a killer monopoly.

STRATEGIC ADVANTAGE 127: Consider using the "good guy/ bad guy" ploy.

If you have ever bought a car from a dealer or made another major purchase in which the salesman had to get the agreed price approved by his boss, you have probably been subjected to the "good guy/bad guy" ploy. It involves a pair of actors, one playing the good guy and the other playing the bad guy, collaborating against you in such a way that to you it appears that you benefit from their squabbling.

This ploy requires a partner, and since most Monopoly players play as individuals (playing Monopoly as part of a team is not the great game it is when played individually), the good guy/bad guy is not often usable. (If you do play Monopoly as part of a team, you should read a book about negotiating. All describe good guy/bad guy techniques.)

A variation of the good guy/bad guy ploy is useful in Monopoly even when you play individually. Invite yourself to join in negotiations between two opponents, when one opponent seems to be on the verge of agreeing to a trade that will hurt your own chances to win. Ally yourself with the weaker opponent. Emphasize the negative ramifications of the deal to your "ally." Point out to your "ally" how your common opponent is getting the better of the deal. Describe how your common opponent is a "bad guy" and how you as a "good guy" can improve your ally's chances of winning by means of an entirely different deal with (who else?) you.

Of course, to make this effective you must be prepared to offer your ally a deal that truly appears to be as beneficial as that offered by the bad guy.

23 🚂

The Second Timing Advantage

One way to look at trading for winning monopolies is as a matter of timing. You previously saw the most important timing advantage—the first timing advantage. That is, you try to get a monopoly just when you are wealthy enough to develop it best, while at the same time allowing opponents to gain a monopoly when they are either too poor or too rich to exploit it fully.

There is a second type of timing advantage. Though not as important as the first timing advantage, it nevertheless increases your chance of winning significantly. The second timing advantage concerns *where* on the board your token rests when monopolies are formed during trades.

The simplest idea behind the second timing advantage is that you should complete a monopoly-forming trade when your opponent is closer to landing on your new monopoly than you are to his or hers.

✻ TACTICAL ADVANTAGE 94: Try to complete monopoly-forming trades at a time when your opponent will probably reach your new monopoly before you reach his or hers.

This advice may seem obvious. However, though all players realize that it is better to be farther from opponents' monopolies, few realize how truly important this is. Many players believe that their token position may be, at worst, a temporary disadvantage, one that will mean little in the long run.

Actually, the second timing advantage is unimportant only during early stages of the game, when no player has enough cash to buy many houses. By the time the monopoly chain reaction occurs, the game is usually "rich" enough so that you must not ignore the second timing advantage.

Figure 23.1 shows the results of 831 experimental games in which the importance of the second timing advantage was tested. Two players with equal cash and property assets formed the Illinois and Marvin Gardens monopolies simultaneously. When the players had an equal chance of landing first on their opponent's monopoly, the player owning the Illinois monopoly won 54 percent of the games. When, however, the Illinois monopoly owner rested on a more distant lot where he was unlikely to be the first to land on his opponent's monopoly, the Illinois monopoly owner won 70 percent of the games. Merely by using the second timing advantage, the Illinois owner improved his winning record from 54 to 70 percent of games played. That is a 29 percent increase in the Illinois owner's winning record—due entirely to the second timing advantage!

FIGURE 23.1

THE SECOND TIMING ADVANTAGE

These games were identical except for the players' locations when the monopolies were formed. In the games in Set A, both players had equal chances of being first to land on their opponent's new monopoly. In Set B, the Marvin Gardens owner was closer to the Illinois monopoly when the monopolies were formed.

	Set A	Set B
Games played	594	227
Games won by Illinois owner	322 (54%)	160 (70%)

DO NOT GET TRAPPED INTO GIVING UP THE SECOND TIMING ADVANTAGE

What should you do when you have an offer for a monopoly-forming trade in which your opponent has the second timing advantage? Since your opponent probably does not realize the real value of the second timing advantage, you can afford to pay whatever is necessary to make your opponent agree to give up the second timing advantage.

Your first alternative (short of simply accepting a second timing disadvantage) is to point out to your trading partner the disadvantage you will suffer. Demand additional cash or property as part of the trade to make up for your token's relatively poor position on the board.

> ✻ **STRATEGIC ADVANTAGE 128:** Demand additional concessions from your trading partner if you are facing a second timing advantage.

Another alternative is to demand an immunity on your partner's new monopoly in exchange for your agreeing to the deal.

> ✻ **STRATEGIC ADVANTAGE 129:** Accept offers for trades involving a second timing disadvantage for yourself (if you must) by demanding an immunity for your landing on your opponent's new monopoly.

Naturally, you should try to get the best immunity deal to which your opponent will agree. In descending order, here are the immunity deals you should try to make:

1. You will pay no (or reduced) rent on your first landing on your opponent's new monopoly.
2. You will pay no (or reduced) rent on any landing you suffer on your opponent's new monopoly during your present circuit of the board.
3. You and your opponent agree to not charge each other rent on a certain number of landings on each other's new monopolies.

Alternative 3 is particularly advantageous because it appears to be a deal that benefits both sides equally while in reality the player with a second timing disadvantage gains by this deal.

A better tactic is to delay completing the deal long enough for the second timing advantage to shift back to you.

> * **STRATEGIC ADVANTAGE 130:** When offered a trading deal creating a killer monopoly with a second timing advantage for your opponent, turn down the offer and agree to the same offer a turn or two later, when you gain back the second timing advantage.

Show general agreement to your opponent's offer, but demand an additional concession to which your opponent will not immediately agree. After a turn or two, when your opponent's second timing advantage has disappeared, you can withdraw your demand for the additional concession. You thus appear generous by making a concession. Your opponent appears to have made no concession but in reality has conceded a second timing advantage.

HIDING THE SECOND TIMING ADVANTAGE

All players can see one another's position on the board, so you can (usually but not always) expect to "pay" something for a second timing advantage. Your opponent may require you to pay by demanding extra cash or property or by simply not accepting your offer. The point of this chapter so far is that you can pay less than the second timing advantage is really worth.

There are more subtle ways to deal with the second timing advantage. Hide the second timing advantage and your opponents may not see it. If you can hide the second timing advantage, you may gain an advantage without having to give up anything whatsoever in return.

MAKE DEALS FROM JAIL

When you are sent to jail, you have the opportunity to gain the second timing advantage quite easily. If you choose to remain in jail for up to three turns, your opponent will likely travel across more than half the board while you do not travel at all. This means that you usually can expect your opponent to reach your new monopoly before you reach his or hers. More important, unless he or she is unusually perceptive, your opponent will not notice how distant you truly are from his or her new monopoly.

✻ TACTICAL ADVANTAGE 95: When you are sent to jail, consider the advantage you gain by closing the deal early during your jail stay.

When your opponent is in jail, the opposite advice is noteworthy.

✻ TACTICAL ADVANTAGE 96: Unless other factors outweigh it, do not close a trade with an opponent who has recently been sent to jail.

BE THE LAST TO MOVE

Another subtle way of gaining a second timing advantage is to be among the last players to move your token after the monopoly chain reaction. An experiment was designed to show how dramatically your results can change depending on whether or not you move first.

A total of 3923 experimental games were played, all involving eight players, all of whom gained a monopoly at the same time. In some of these games, Player 5, who owned the Illinois monopoly, was always the first to move after the monopoly chain reaction. In other games, all eight players shared equally the task of rolling the dice first. The results of this experiment are shown in Figure 23.2. Not being the player who moves first after the monopoly chain reaction results in dramatic improvements in the percentage of games won. The improvement increases as the amount of liquid assets in the game increases from a moderate to a high amount.

To put this information to profitable use, simply remember to finish trades after your roll of the dice—not before.

✳ **TACTICAL ADVANTAGE 97:** Roll the dice and move your token before making a trade that forms monopolies.

If you have doubts about the legality of Tactical Advantage 97, review Monopoly Myth 8 in Chapter 3.

WHEN TO COMPLETE MONOPOLY-FORMING TRADES

The strong side of the board is the side that can cost you the most rent. When monopolies are formed early in the game, the strong sides of the board are generally the first and second sides of the board. When monopolies are formed well after all the properties have been sold, the third or fourth sides of the board are the strong sides.

FIGURE 23.2

THE EFFECT OF MOVING FIRST AFTER
THE MONOPOLY CHAIN REACTION

	Player 5 Always Moves First	Player Moving First Selected Randomly
Games played—Moderate liquid assets	1322	641
Games won by Player 5	141 (10.6%)	94 (14.7%)
Improvement for Player 5	—	+38.7%
Games played—High liquid assets	943	1017
Games won by Player 5	95 (10%)	192 (18.9%)
Improvement for Player 5	—	+89%

It is to your advantage to create monopolies while you are resting toward the end of the strong side of the board. Doing so means that you will enter the weak sides of the board on your next move. Following this advice increases your chances of winning by 5 to 60 percent when there are many monopolies on the board.

＊**TACTICAL ADVANTAGE 98:** When there are or soon will be many monopolies, complete monopoly-forming trades when you are on the verge of entering the weak side of the board.

24

The Psychology of Luck

Suppose you play a dice game in which throwing an odd number is a success. Suppose you play long enough to finally have seven odd-number successes in a row. What will probably happen if you immediately toss the dice three more times? Here are the most popular answers:

1. You will probably roll two or three odds, because when you're hot, you're hot.
2. You will probably roll two or three evens, because the law of averages says that unusual events (like seven odds in a row) tend to get neutralized.
3. You will roll close to 1½ evens, because that is what the probability formula predicts.

Here are the results of such a game in which the dice were tossed just over 2 million times (a machine "tossed" the dice, as doing it by hand would take over a year):

Number of dice tosses	2,000,094	
Number of times seven odds occurred in a row	7461	
Number of times seven odds were followed by three more odds	914	(12.25%)
Number of times seven odds were followed by three evens	926	(12.41%)

Number of times seven odds were followed		
by a combination of odds and evens	5621	(75.33%)
Number of odds after seven odds in a row	11,158	(49.85%)
Number of evens after seven odds in a row	11,225	(50.15%)

Apparently, the dice didn't care whether there had been seven previous odds. The results are just what probability would predict.

Anyone who truly believes that what happened in the past could affect what happens in a future dice toss would have to believe that dice have some way of remembering the past and that a die has a will and a way to carry out its will.

Even people who know positively that dice have no memory and that inanimate objects have no plans for the future occasionally let their emotions overpower logic. They form feelings and expectations about uncertain future events on the basis of what has happened in the recent past. People who form such feelings often may be called luck-conscious. The important fact to appreciate is that luck-conscious people constitute the majority of the population!

It is not rare for luck-conscious players to get strong feelings about luck because even ordinary, average luck contains sporadic periods of unusually bad luck and unusually good luck.

A man who tells you he is in the middle of a lucky streak is not really telling you anything about the dice or cards or probability, even though he may think he is. He is telling you about his perception of a situation and about his frame of mind.

It is wise to be sensitive to this. The receptiveness of a luck-conscious player to one of your offers depends in part on his or her frame of mind.

A player who feels lucky will probably not want anything in the game to change; such a player is predisposed to reject any offer from you before even starting to evaluate it seriously.

In contrast, the player who feels unlucky or who is pessimistic about the course of the game is predisposed to accept change. A trade deal proposal from anyone is an opportunity for change. An offer directed to such a player is likely to find a receptive mind.

✳ **STRATEGIC ADVANTAGE 131:** Pay attention to statements indicating what a player thinks about a current bout of bad luck or any pessimism about his or her prospects in the game.

Such instances are a good time to approach that player about a deal.

Some players remain tight-lipped about how they think their luck is running. In such cases you must judge opponents' luck by what they do rather than what they say. Look for a couple of consecutive landings on Income Tax or a series of landings on opponents' property. Recent bad luck tends to cause players to be more receptive toward a change in the game.

> ✱ **STRATEGIC ADVANTAGE 132:** If you have the freedom to offer deals at any time, do so immediately after one or more bad things have happened to the player with whom you will negotiate.

CLASSIFIED ADVICE FOR MEN AND WOMEN

Research has indicated that all people have misperceptions about the role of luck but that the nature of the misperception depends on sex. In recognition of that, there follows here a section directed to women, which men can skip, and a section for men, which women can skip.

Advice for Women

Women place more importance on the role of luck than men do, according to a number of scientific studies. Acknowledging the role of luck is useful, because luck is a reality. Women succeed better than men in activities where it is important to build a margin of safety against uncertainties.

But overestimating luck can be a handicap. One study showed that women's sports teams are not as likely as men's teams to come from behind to win. Believing their team's luck was bad, female players resigned themselves to defeat before the game was over.

If you are in the process of losing a Monopoly game, do not despair about your luck; instead, start to negotiate and change the game. You probably have more control over the outcome than you believe.

Advice for Men

Men repeatedly fail to recognize and fail to make allowance in their plans for the role of luck, the uncertainties that affect everything from games to wars. Not acknowledging the role of luck in sports and games causes performance to be erratic. After building a lead in a game, men assume it was due to their superior strategy and performance under pressure, and men thus tend to relax and allow opponents to catch up.

If you are winning a Monopoly game, do not assume that you have the ability to continue doing so. Build up a margin of safety, in case some of your good fortune was due to luck, which you simply failed to recognize.

25 🚂

Your Winning Strategy

You faced the secret behind your best winning strategy earlier in this book if you appreciated the difference between the probability of an "either-or event" and the probability of an "and event." Your best strategy for winning Monopoly is to use many "either-or" events and to avoid using "and" events.

An example of a strategy based on "and" events is, "I'll wait until I have $1000; then I'll get the Illinois monopoly by trading with Joe." The success of this strategy depends on Joe's reaction *and* on what other players offer Joe *and* on what light monopolies are manufactured early *and* on what heavier monopolies are formed *and* on other events and conditions. Calculate the probability of any sequence of "and" events, and you always find a tiny number.

Such strategies are unnecessary and unwise. It is possible to play Monopoly using "either-or" events with all "and" events couched within the "either-or" events so that failure of any one event does not ruin an entire game plan. Simply stated, the best strategy for winning Monopoly follows:

A1. Aim to get the first killer monopoly, Connecticut, if you own one of the lots. Connecticut is your first ideal monopoly. If you do not own a lot, go to step B.

A2. Review the trading alternatives of any opponent who owns part of your ideal monopoly. Consider simple swaps, compound swaps, and group trades.

A3. When considering a trade involving Connecticut or Virginia, use the three-house rule and your knowledge about weak sisters to determine whether you can acquire your preferred monopoly without creating an opposing monopoly strong enough to challenge yours.

A4. When considering a trade that forms for you an upper-tier monopoly, use the three-house rule to evaluate trades giving an opponent a lower-tier monopoly. When evaluating a trade forming two upper-tier monopolies, use the hotel rule. Keep in mind the weak sisters.

A5. Evaluate trade possibilities in order from the most distant monopoly to the one nearest the monopoly you want to get, keeping in mind your negotiating power with each opponent with whom you would have to deal and keeping in mind whether a player is wealthier than you.

A6. When you identify a suitable trading partner, set trade objectives, including how much you are willing to concede to your trading partner, taking into account your I2 wealth predictor factor. The greater your wealth, the less you need to concede.

A7. If you do not find a suitable trading partner or if your best efforts to negotiate a trade do not succeed within your trading window, act unconcerned and go on to step B.

A8. If you do gain a killer monopoly, build houses and hotels as your first priority. The second priority is either to block or build additional monopolies, depending on whether you own an upper-tier or a lower-tier monopoly. Identify stars and supporting players.

B. Determine your next ideal monopoly (and your trading window) by calculating your liquid assets and determining which is the *least* expensive monopoly on which you can almost build three houses. As your next ideal monopoly to acquire, it is your new power center. If you can gain own-ership of a monopoly at your power center, you know it is safe to give an equally rich opponent any lighter, low-tier monopoly and it is safe to give any equally rich opponent an upper-tier monopoly. (Continue as from step A2.)

* **STRATEGIC ADVANTAGE 133:** Keep track of your ideal monop-oly at every point in the game. These are your power centers. Do not ignore any trade possibility that will give you a killer monopoly at your power center.

THE POWER CENTER

Following the strategy just described provides seven separate op-portunities to succeed—one opportunity to win at each of seven "or" events.

Each of the power centers arises in sequence from Connecticut to Virginia to New York to Boardwalk to Illinois to Marvin Gardens to Pennsylvania. The most important advantage of aiming for each of these monopolies in sequence is that if you fail to gain your power-center monopoly, you must only wait awhile for your liquid assets to build. You soon will have a new power center and another opportunity to gain a game-winning monopoly.

LIGHT MONOPOLIES FIRST

The strategy outlined here, aiming for each monopoly in sequence, results in the formation of more light killer monopolies and rela-tively fewer heavy, upper-tier monopolies. There are several rea-sons this is advantageous.

First, there is less demand or competition for the lighter mo-nopolies, so you have more bargaining power.

Second, you may recall from the graph of the results of the eight-monopoly tournament (Figure 20.6) that the lower-tier monopolies dominated their ideal portions of the game more strongly than any upper-tier monopoly ever dominated its part of the game. Lower-tier monopolies, when formed at an appropriate time, are simply harder to beat.

Third, when you aim for an upper-tier monopoly, you run a major risk while you wait for your liquid assets to build. Opponents may form lower-tier monopolies, destroying your ability to continue to build your liquid assets.

Fourth, following the sequential strategy tends to give you one of the first monopolies formed. Besides increasing your income earlier than most opponents, you gain more room to maneuver. That is, you have more trading alternatives. Once monopolies are formed, the remaining property combinations that can form monopolies shrink. The chances of compound swaps and group trades drop drastically.

Finally, if your heart is set on a high-rent, heavy monopoly, consider the fact that if you play a light monopoly properly, you can, through opponents' bankruptcies, gain a heavy monopoly eventually in any case.

HOW TO BRING CONNECTICUT AND VIRGINIA INTO THE GAME AS POWER CENTERS

One difficulty with trying to win with Connecticut or Virginia is that many players will not trade for monopolies until all or nearly all properties have been sold. By the time this happens, the best time to develop these monopolies may have passed. Figure 9.3 showed that the liquid assets of an average player at 150 moves, when the last property is sold, on average, exceeds $1800, not too rich for Virginia but beyond Connecticut's ideal time.

An effective way to handle this problem is to deal for mutual property options before all properties are sold. A mutual property option is an agreement to sell an opponent a certain property if you are the first player to land on it. In exchange, your opponent agrees to sell you a property you would like to have if he or she lands on it before you do.

MONOPOLY'S BEST TRADE DEAL

If you manage to buy a lot or two on a light color group, try to arrange a mutual property option whereby you can buy from an opponent another lot on a light monopoly.

> * **STRATEGIC ADVANTAGE 134:** Arrange a mutual property option that gains you lots in a light monopoly.

Most players will accept such deals if they gain the "better," more expensive property. However, since all properties will be landed on early in the game, when only light-monopoly houses can be built in significant numbers, you are likely to gain a monopoly near your power center, while your opponent gains a monopoly with which he or she can do little. This trade can result in a quick, runaway win for you.

MONOPOLIES TO CHOOSE IF YOU ARE BEHIND

It has been pointed out that if you are less wealthy than opponents, you must trade for monopolies early to have a reasonable chance of winning. This usually means getting Connecticut or Virginia.

Experimental games have proved that Boardwalk is a particularly good choice for a cash-poor player. With Boardwalk, the most inconsistent monopoly, a little streak of good luck can enable you to make a big comeback.

Boardwalk's inconsistency makes it a poor choice for players who are doing well, because a little streak of bad luck can ruin an otherwise successful game.

HOW TO CONTROL THE TEMPO OF TRADING

Sometimes your luck can be so bad that when you look for monopoly manufacturing opportunities, all you find is a solitary chance for an upper-tier monopoly. If opponents have opportunities for lighter monopolies, you have a problem. Opponents who trade among themselves to form monopolies while you wait for your liquid assets to grow sufficiently choke your chances for a win.

In such a situation you need to discourage all opponents from trading. Obviously, the fact that you yourself do not present any trade proposals is one factor discouraging trading. In fact, you might consider not even offering tactical trade proposals to avoid establishing a trading precedent.

    ✳ **STRATEGIC ADVANTAGE 135:** When you must discourage all strategic trading, refrain from tactical trading as well.

In addition, you can take active steps to prevent trading. To determine what these steps might be, consider when and why Monopoly players trade or do not trade.

Players do not trade because negotiating is more stressful than assembling a monopoly by simply rolling dice, and early in the game players do not have enough cash to do much with a monopoly. Once there are no more properties to buy and there is enough cash to handle emergencies, the game can, within a few circuits of the board, become routine. Trading for monopolies, while relatively stressful, will likely become preferable to monotony.

The first thing you can do to prevent monotony and the accompanying trading is to provide "entertainment." Replenish supplies of snacks and drinks, if it is in your power to do so. Introduce jokes, stories, or general conversation.

A more immediate way to provide entertainment is to give all players a stake, a self-interest, in continuing to circle the board. Introduce game-related bets or wagers relating to future results of players' moves or landings.

    ✳ **STRATEGIC ADVANTAGE 136:** When you want players to delay making trades for monopolies, introduce bets or wagers involving future moves and landings to give players more reason to continue to circle the board and/or to preoccupy their attention.

When aiming to develop an upper-tier monopoly, you want to delay trading until the 225-move, 38-circuit, $1500-cash milestone, so it makes sense to key in the predictions and bets you make to that point in the game. Here are examples of such bets:

1. The number of landings on a particular square (such as Go to Jail) in a specified number of circuits

2. Player wealth rankings at the end of specified time (use the I2 wealth predictor)
3. Who will be first (or last) to again have $1500 cash
4. How many (if any) players will throw three doubles to go to jail before all players have $1500 cash
5. Whether or not the first Chance card will again surface before Player X has $1500 cash
6. How much cash Player X will collect from Community Chest or Chance cards

If you remember some of the data presented thus far in this book, you can not only delay opponents from forming monopolies, but you can earn a few Monopoly dollars as well.

PART FIVE

OPTIONAL TECHNIQUES FOR WORLD-CLASS PLAYERS

If you know how to put into practice all the elements of the sequential power-center strategy described in Chapter 25, you can play competitively with any player, including the national champions who gather each year in Atlantic City to determine the world champion. Having read this book, you should know no less about Monopoly than world-class players.

Assurance of being competitive is not a guarantee of being a world-class player. This book, like any book, can yield knowledge, but not skill. The formula for transforming superior knowledge into superior skill involves measures of experience, effort, and aptitude as well as of knowledge.

The principal advantage of superior skill is that it forces opponents to accumulate greater amounts of luck to win. Extraordinary luck is by definition rare, so highly skilled players lose less often. Even so, no player is immune from losing. Superior skill can overcome a pound of bad luck, but not a whole barrelful.

Since those who have read this far should already be competitive with all players, Part Five is optional. Those who wish to play or do play at a world-class level should go on to the last part of this book. Such players will find the advice in Chapter 28 particularly important.

26 🚂

How to Deceive Your Opponents Honestly

Your playing partners must, of course, accept some of your deals and bets for you to benefit by them. This chapter describes a few, little known, psychological ploys you can use to further help get your opponents to do what you propose to them during negotiations.

ATTRIBUTION

Attribution refers to the fact that people's guesses or estimates about the probability of an event are proportional to their ability to imagine or visualize that event. For example, if you simply ask, "What are the chances of sinking down deep into the ground while taking a walk?" a person will reply that the probability is one in a million or some other very low probability. Suppose instead that you asked the same question this way: "What is the chance of walking into quicksand or walking into an open manhole or into a huge water-filled pothole or into a loosely filled excavated hole or into a poorly covered construction trench?" Asked this way, people's estimates of the likelihood of events are likely to be much higher.

The reason for this is that the second question leads the listener to draw mind pictures. The wording made it possible for the listener to visualize possible events. Researchers have found that making it possible to visualize an event causes people to overestimate greatly the chances of that event's occurrence.

It is not hard to see the effects of attribution in everyday life. Statistically, traveling by air is safer than any other method. Yet it is so easy to imagine air crashes that airplane travelers tend to overestimate the risk and thus suffer more sweaty palms than other travelers.

You can use the attribution phenomenon to help get your playing partners to accept your offers for trades and other deals by making them appear more attractive. How to do this may be best shown by example.

Suppose you want Player B to accept taking immunity on your Illinois monopoly. In exchange you would get one of his properties. To close this deal you need to get Player B to appreciate fully (or more than fully) the value of the immunity that you will give him.

Make it easy for Player B to visualize himself landing on your Illinois monopoly. Instead of saying, "I'll give you immunity on the Illinois monopoly," say, "I'll give you immunity on each of three red properties, Kentucky, Indiana, and Illinois, no matter how often you pass by and land. And if you draw the Chance card that says 'go to Illinois,' your immunity protects you too. Without immunity, each time you land you'd pay up to $1100 in cold, hard cash." While you are saying that you could use your finger to mimic a token counting out the squares and landing on each of the red properties.

* **TACTICAL ADVANTAGE 99:** When you want another player to overestimate the probability of certain events, spell out those events with your finger on the board or with other gestures. Describe the events in detail; most important, describe all the ways the events could occur. Use descriptive language.

* **TACTICAL ADVANTAGE 100:** When you want another player to underestimate the probability of certain events, point out the events as plainly as possible. Do not point out any fact drawing attention to the properties. Do not gesture or point to those properties.

THE CONDITIONAL CORRELATION SYNDROME

Related to attribution, though a little more complicated, is another psychological trait, the conditional correlation syndrome.

Before seeing what exactly it is, try the following quiz, which is an example of how the conditional correlation syndrome works.

Take this statement as true: Joannie has finally met the man of her dreams—a real athlete.

Which of the following items is most likely true about Joannie's new boyfriend? (1) He is tall. (2) He is tall and strong. (3) He is tall, strong, and muscular. (4) He is tall, strong, muscular, and very bright.

Most people answer this quiz with item 3. Their idea is that there is a strong correlation between being tall, strong, and muscular and being athletic, whereas being smart is not so well correlated with athletes.

The correct answer is choice 1—that he is merely tall. If you answered incorrectly, you were a victim of the conditional correlation syndrome.

The correct answer involves the probability of "and" events. The group of athletes who are tall, strong, and muscular is necessarily smaller than the group that is merely tall. In a group of 1000 athletes, those who are tall number less than 1000, say 800. Of those 800, those who are also strong is again smaller, say 750, and so on.

It does not matter if being strong is more common among athletes than is being tall. It is impossible for the tall and strong to outnumber the tall. Mathematicians say that the tall and strong group is a subset of the "tall" group. The tall, strong, and muscular group is a subset of a subset.

In general, people recognize that the probability of two events happening together is smaller than the probability of either event occurring by itself. Still, people tend to overestimate the probability of the events occurring together. The conditional correlation syndrome refers to the fact that people tend to overestimate most severely the probability of two events occurring together when the events are correlated.

You can easily put the conditional correlation syndrome into many of your Monopoly deals, for two reasons: First, many Monopoly deals can be tied into dice throws in some way. Second, most players know that mid-size dice throws such as 6, 7, and 8 are more likely than extremely high or low numbers; that is, most players see a correlation between likely events and mid-size dice rolls.

> * **TACTICAL ADVANTAGE 101:** When you need to offer a player a deal involving one uncertain event, put that event in combination with a second event correlated with the first.

Suppose you need to offer an opponent, Player B, immunity on your Illinois (red) monopoly to get something valuable in exchange. To make the immunity seem more valuable to your opponents, you can offer the immunity in combination with a correlated event, say, when Player B lands on your monopoly on a dice roll of 5, 6, 7, 8, or 9.

Many people feel that the probability of two events in combination when both events are usually tied to each other is greater than the probability of either alone. Many people will assume that if the probability of landing on the red monopoly is ½, the probability of a 5, 6, 7, 8, or 9 dice roll in combination with landing on the red monopoly is greater than ½.

Using the conditional correlation syndrome is a way to give away less while appearing to give away more and, alternatively, to take more while appearing to take less.

UNCERTAINTY REPULSION

Another trait people share about uncertain events is a strong desire for absolute certainty or absolute impossibility. People like the certainty of good events and the impossibility of bad events. They will pay a dear price to remove the last few percentage points that separate a probability from absolute certainty (probability = 1) and absolute impossibility (probability = 0).

Researchers have found that people are willing to pay more to increase their chances from 90 to 100 percent than they would pay for this same 10 percent increase of from 60 to 70 percent. The same trend holds true for undesired events in the 1 to 19 percent range; people are willing to pay a great deal to remove the last few percentage points of uncertainty.

To take advantage of this trait, try to offer deals that have either very high or very low probabilities.

A prime example of such a deal is the possibility of a double landing on a monopoly in one pass. A player who lands on Oriental and then throws a 2 or a 3 will land on the Connecticut monopoly twice in a single pass. The probability of such a double landing is low—about 1 percent. It is easy to calculate the expected value of this combination of events: it is about $8 per circuit.

You can offer to reduce this risk to zero by offering a rent immunity for the second landing. If you do not expect the game to last a very long time, you will likely find a player to accept such a deal with a healthy profit margin for you.

Another potential high-profit deal is to sell an immunity against one of your opponents' being sent to a property you own by a "go to" Chance card. (Illinois Avenue, St. Charles Place, and Boardwalk are prime candidates for such a deal.)

> * TACTICAL ADVANTAGE 102: Offer deals that reduce low probabilities to zero or increase high probabilities to 100 percent. Players will pay a premium price for such deals.

ASSUMPTIONS OF RISKS AND CONTROL

Have you ever wondered why people are willing to tolerate some risks more than others? Why is it that many people who are willing to smoke, drink, ride bicycles, or go skiing will not tolerate other risks that experts say are objectively much smaller, such as breathing polluted air or eating food with additives. Smoking a single pack of cigarettes has the same effect on life expectancy as drinking the much-maligned water of Miami for over 14 years. While everyone decries the water pollution risk, almost one-third of the population voluntarily takes the smoking risk.

Risk experts have identified control as a primary determinant of how much risk is tolerated. Having control is why the driver of a car feels safer than do his passengers. Conversely, not having control over the air we breathe makes us intolerant of the air pollution risk.

One study showed that people who picked their own lottery numbers (thus giving them more control) made them feel they had a better chance of winning than did lottery players who could not select their number.

You can use this idea about control to make your trade offers seem more attractive to your partners. Offer them a choice when you can. For example, instead of offering a player Boardwalk and Kentucky in exchange for a property that will give you a monopoly, offer a choice of any two of four properties. The selection might include Boardwalk, Kentucky, Oriental, and Virginia. The end result may be exactly the same as your original offer of Boardwalk and Kentucky. But by offering a selection, you will make the offer more attractive and thus increase the chances that the offer will be accepted.

* TACTICAL ADVANTAGE 103: Give your deal partners a sense of control by offering them a choice. This will make them feel better about the merits of your offer.

LOSSES LOOM LARGER THAN GAINS

People tend to worry more about losing what they have than about missing opportunities for equivalently large gains. Studies show that few people will take a big risk to get a big gain, but many people will take a big risk to avert a loss. In short, potential losses have more impact than potential gains.

If you offer a choice between possibly gaining $1000 and possibly avoiding a $1000 loss, most players will probably choose the latter.

That is why your opponent is reluctant to trade properties when both parties gain monopolies of quite equal value. The prospect of paying huge rents on one monopoly will loom larger in your opponent's mind than the prospect of collecting equivalently large rents from the other.

This can be a problem because many of the most important trades you need to make potentially involve both big gains and big losses. You can expect the player to choose to avoid the big loss, and to do that he or she must turn down the trade.

To make such double-sided offers seem more acceptable, talk about any gains your partner could expect from the deal in terms of avoiding losses. You can do this by talking about the new monopoly as if the deal had already taken place and by referring to the future rents as money the player would "lose out on" by rejecting the offer. An example is, "If you accept my offer and take Indiana Avenue, you won't lose about $1000 each time somebody lands on Kentucky, and you won't lose about $1000 each time someone lands on Illinois."

＊STRATEGIC ADVANTAGE 137: When negotiating the creation of two monopolies, describe future rents a trading partner may receive as payments this player will avoid losing.

You should also note that many players do not realize that when they simultaneously get and give monopolies through a trade they will pay additional rent to one player but will probably collect rent from a number of players. A reminder about this might push the deal through.

27

Anomalies

Monopoly anomalies are situations involving unusual tactics or strategy. Due to their rarity, you probably have not given these situations much thought.

BUILDING SHORTAGES

The rules limit players to 32 houses and 12 hotels. Since four houses go back to the bank whenever a hotel is built, there can be up to 12 hotels plus four houses each on eight additional lots. This is more than sufficient for most games.

When there is a shortage, the rules require players to bid for houses as they become available. This is a greater hardship for owners of light monopolies, as they must outbid players who have more rent to gain from each house.

On the other hand, light-monopoly owners, because they need less money to buy and sell houses, are in a better position to take advantage of building shortages and of near building shortages.

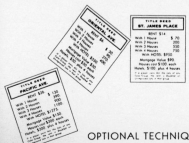

Suppose buildings are arranged as follows:

PLAYER	MONOPOLY	BUILDINGS
A	Baltic	2 hotels
A	Connecticut	3 hotels
B	Virginia	6 houses
B	New York	lots owned by A and B
B	Illinois	9 houses
B	Marvin Gardens	9 houses
C	Pennsylvania	3 hotels
C	Boardwalk	2 hotels
B	4 Railroads	
A	2 Utilities	
TOTAL:		10 hotels, 24 houses

Player A will eventually go bankrupt, as her expected rent income falls far short of rents she will pay to her opponents. And if Player B builds houses or builds hotels, Player A's prospects will become bleak even faster.

If Player A is alert, it may occur to her to sell two of her hotels, leaving her with four houses on two of her monopolized lots. This leaves four hotels in the bank, but no houses. This move prevents both opponents from building any more houses. (Even if Player B had enough cash to buy hotels, he could not do so, as it is necessary to buy four houses before buying a hotel.)

Suppose, furthermore, that Players B and C are heavily mortgaged and have little cash cushion, which is the situation in which heavy-monopoly owners usually find themselves.

If Player C must sell a house to pay a $15 poor tax, he would have to sell two hotels! There are no houses, so he must sell his Boardwalk hotel as a unit. This leaves a hotel on Park Place and no buildings on Boardwalk, which is contrary to the rules. This means that he must immediately sell the Park Place hotel too. To pay a $15 debt, Player C had to sell $2000 of buildings at half price.

Suppose that Player B is unaware of the building shortage. Player A can offer Player B a lot that will give Player B the New York monopoly. In exchange, Player A receives cash and all four Railroads. As Player B cannot build houses on his new monopoly or on any existing property, Player A has succeeded in improving her position tremendously.

* **TACTICAL ADVANTAGE 104:** Keep in mind the mortgaging and building problems you can cause opponents who neglect to monitor the number of houses and hotels on the board.

It is not unheard of for a Monopoly player to include buildings from a second Monopoly set and for the set owner to "forget" to mention this fact until all 32 genuine houses are on the board.

NATURAL KILLER MONOPOLIES

In games involving many players, it is rare for a player to get a monopoly by the roll of dice. When it happens, the lucky owner immediately becomes the player to beat. The lucky player is actually unlucky, however, if he has drawn a heavy monopoly. All players' liquid assets during the property acquisition stage are insufficient to develop a heavy monopoly. Concurrently, all opponents feel threatened and engage in furious trading as soon as all other natural monopolies are destroyed. Some of the manufactured monopolies are invariably closer to the power center than is the natural monopoly. As a result, the lucky player soon becomes an underdog.

The solution is to trade away your heavy natural monopoly. Some of your opponents are liable to think you have lost your mind, but in return for your natural monopoly you can demand and get from your trading partner almost any group of properties you want. With your pick of properties you should easily be able to manufacture a monopoly of your own and reinstate your initial status as the favorite to win the game.

* **STRATEGIC ADVANTAGE 138:** Trade away a heavy natural monopoly unless you have perfect veto power over other killer monopolies.

A HAPPY DECISION:
WHICH MONOPOLY TO DEVELOP FIRST

When blessed with two monopolies, the question immediately arises as to the first monopoly on which houses should be built. The correct answer presupposes that when you develop one monopoly right after another, you do so in the most advantageous manner.

You should build three houses per lot on the first monopoly, followed by three houses per lot on the second monopoly. The return on your investment falls off dramatically after you have erected three houses per lot.

> *TACTICAL ADVANTAGE 105: You should build three houses per lot on the first monopoly followed by three houses per lot on the heavier monopoly followed by hotels on the first monopoly followed by hotels on the second.

The question of which monopoly to develop first boils down to the following: Which monopoly offers the higher marginal real return on the money invested in houses, assuming three houses per lot?

Calculating in your head marginal real rates of return can be cumbersome. It is easier simply to follow a few rules of thumb. This is particularly true since using the rents printed on the Title Deed cards yields basic marginal ROIs instead of real marginal ROIs.

The first rule of thumb is to develop first the heaviest monopoly for which you can immediately buy three houses per lot. This is simply an offshoot of the three-house rule and the hotel rule.

> *TACTICAL ADVANTAGE 106: Invest first in the monopoly in which you can become fully invested by buying up to three houses per lot. There is one exception: Never develop Baltic first.

If you cannot afford to buy as many as three houses per lot on any monopoly, follow instead the same rule suggested previously for judging the real value of alternative individual properties. That is, invest in the property closest to Free Parking.

✻ TACTICAL ADVANTAGE 107: Given a choice of monopolies in which to invest less than three houses per lot, invest first in the monopoly closest to Free Parking. Continue to invest in that monopoly until reaching three houses per lot. Then invest in the monopoly you own that is next closest to Free Parking.

Tactical Advantage 107 carries the assumption Boardwalk is on Free Parking. If you own both the Boardwalk and New York monopolies, however, develop New York first. You will recall that New York is always a stronger monopoly than Boardwalk.

The above rules vary slightly from the general advice to invest first in the properties with highest marginal real ROIs, but the variance is too small to be of concern.

DISREGARD SUNK COSTS AND AVOID ENTRAPMENT

Business books discuss the need not to be blinded by "sunk costs"; psychology texts refer to the same idea as avoiding "entrapment." Whatever it is called, you should beware of clinging to a course of action simply because you have in the past put time, money, or effort into it. Doing so serves psychological purposes but no useful economic purpose.

Instances in Monopoly when it might be necessary to disregard sunk costs include these:

1. Abandon your efforts to develop your monopoly and trade for another monopoly.
2. Sell houses at half price so that you can trade away a monopoly.
3. Develop monopolies only partially in favor of a second monopoly.
4. Set aside your negotiation stance if it is not working.

HOW TO WIN MONOPOLIZED STALEMATED GAMES

Monopoly stalemates usually involve games in which no player is able to trade for a killer monopoly. An interesting, effective way to deal with such a situation was described in Chapter 2.

On rare occasions you and your last opponents will stalemate, despite the fact that there are a number of killer monopolies in the game. You do not want to play the same game forever, yet you do not want to call such a game a tie.

Here is a way to turn such a stalemate into an outright win.

First, make certain you truly are in a stalemated game. Calculate each player's expected rent income and rent expenses using the expected-value formula. If normal cash flow ($171 per circuit of the board) is larger than any player's deficit between expected rent income and rent expenses, you are truly in a stalemated game. (If the expected-value formula indicates that you will eventually go bankrupt, you may decide that calling the game a draw is the best you can do.)

If you are truly in a stalemated game, suggest that all players give back all their cash to the bank except for pocket money, say, $500, and that all players abide by the results of this shortened game.

For reasons having to do with a statistical measure called a standard deviation, the winner of such a game will usually be the player whose monopolies congregate most closely around the Free Parking square. (For this purpose consider Boardwalk as being in its actual location, just before Go.)

Of course, if your monopolies are not as close to Free Parking as your opponents', there is no good reason to offer this proposal. Also, when proposing this solution to a stalemated game, you must make sure you do not suffer a second timing disadvantage.

28 🚂

Execute!

Becoming an excellent Monopoly player requires the same thing necessary to achieve excellence in most other activities—practice. You must translate your ideas and knowledge into the practical ability to execute. Fortunately, practicing Monopoly poses no burden; the final advantages presented in this book are entirely pleasant.

* TACTICAL ADVANTAGE 108: Practice executing effective tactics by playing Monopoly.

* STRATEGIC ADVANTAGE 139: Practice executing effective strategy by playing Monopoly.

The only obstacle to playing Monopoly often is finding a group of people with the time to play. Even this difficulty is removed if you have a home computer, as several computerized versions of Monopoly have been developed. These allow you to compete alone against any number of "electronic brains." These programs also take care of the "bookkeeping" in games you play with human opponents.

The computer software used to play the games described in this book is available under the title "Automated Banker" for the line of computers manufactured by Commodore.

TECHNICAL VERSUS HUMAN SKILLS

The need to practice to improve execution applies mainly to the technical (gameboard) side of the game. Though the human factors side is also improvable through practice, skill in human factors improves independently of playing Monopoly; that is, it seems to improve naturally with age. Thus Monopoly can be welcomed to the list of things that we can always do better as we get older.